D1477724

Spatial Recall:
MEMORY IN ARCHITECTURE AND LANDSCAPE

MARC TREIB, EDITOR

Whether intended or not, architecture and designed landscapes serve as grand mnemonic devices that record and transmit vital aspects of culture and history. Architects and landscape architects have addressed the idea of externalized memory in differing ways at different times, varying from the "emulation" characteristic of classicism to its nearly complete repudiation by modernist practice. Over the last decades the gradient between these two poles has fluctuated once again, however, bringing us consciously memory-laden projects such as New Urbanism, postmodern historicism, ecological remediation, and activist historic preservation.

The contributors to *Spatial Recall* cast a broad net over the concept of memory, taken here as the trace of all that has gone before, whether existing as tangible remains or as a vague yet lingering mental presence. With a variety of perspectives, the authors—scholars, practicing designers, and artists—treat broad topics like message and audience and more specific issues concerning the production of design. Several address the idea of nature or cities as a whole, others discuss buildings taken as fragments; others suggest that the manner in which a building is designed can stimulate the production of memories. As a structured set of essays, *Spatial Recall* offers a comprehensive view of memory in the built environment, how we have read it in the past, and how we can create it in the future.

Spatial Recall:

Spatial Recall:

Spatial Recall:

MEMORY IN ARCHITECTURE AND LANDSCAPE

Spatial Recall:

MARC TREIB, EDITOR

MEMORY IN ARCHITECTURE AND LANDSCAPE

 Routledge
Taylor & Francis Group

NEW YORK AND LONDON

First published 2009 by Routledge
270 Madison Avenue, New York, NY 10016

Simultaneously published in the UK by Routledge
2 Park Square, Milton Park, Abingdon, Oxon OX14 4RN

Routledge is an imprint of the Taylor & Francis Group,
an informa business

Designed by Marc Treib
Typeset in Trump Medieval and Syntax
Printed and bound in Great Britain by
TJ International Ltd, Padstow, Cornwall

British Library Cataloging in Publication Data
A catalog record for this book is available from
the British Library

Library of Congress Cataloging-in-Publication Data
A catalog record for this book has been applied for

ISBN10 0-415-77735-6 (hbk)
ISBN10 0-415-77736-4 (pbk)

ISBN13 978-0-415-77735-3 (hbk)
ISBN13 978-0-415-77736-0 (pbk)

for Karen Madsen and John Furlong

Yes, Now
I Remember:
An Introduction

Marc Treib

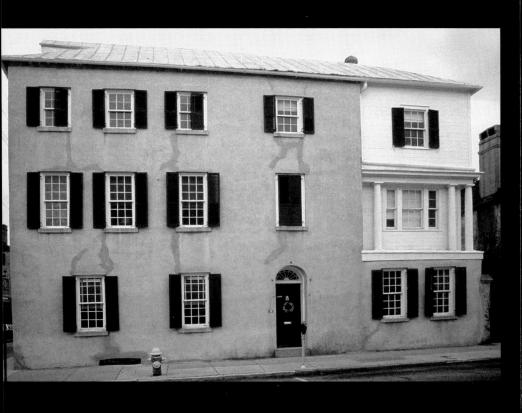

In his 1972 film *Roma*, Federico Fellini lucidly illustrates the collective nightmares shared by the engineer, the builder, the cinéaste, and the archaeologist. While tunneling for a new subway line through the soil beneath Rome, the great digging machine is brought to a stop as it encounters a huge hall lined with murals from ancient times. The builder and the film crew hesitantly enter through a small rent in the wall and stand in awe of the painted figures who seem to be looking at them. And then, without warning, the frescoes begin to disintegrate before their very eyes—the air entering the hall from the tunneling catalyzes a chemical reaction that is destroying the pigments. The intruders stand fixed and horrified, but there is nothing to be done—the process is rapid, and irreversible. The destruction of these ancient images has erased these likenesses, their histories, and the memories that accompany them. What part of the heritage has been lost will not be ascertained. We will never know—or forget—these someones, somethings; these memories have vanished in the clear, modern air.

We put in writing thoughts otherwise lost to time. Writing externalizes and makes concrete; writing allows us to add, subtract, and overlay; to shape and to polish. Writing, however, is essentially linear and restricted to the specific codes shared by speaker or writer, and listener or reader. We can only imagine the degree to which the complexity increases when we consider the environment as a whole, and its potential for storing and aiding in the retrieval of memory—a subject masterfully explored by Frances Yates in her classic study *The Art of Memory* from 1974.[1] Unlike writing, however, our built world may choose not to engage communication or memory as its primary vocation, yet it records and transmits history nonetheless. And while I would not claim—as some others have—that our built environment functions literally as a text or a narrative, certain aspects of architecture, landscape architecture, and art works do share selected characteristics with texts. Foremost among these are the ability to express ideas and attitudes, and at times, to communicate them with an acceptable degree of comprehension. Memories remain embedded in the form, remain to be unearthed, read, and decoded—however imperfectly or incorrectly. Memories may

[0-1]
HOUSE WITH ADDITIONS, CHARLESTON, SOUTH CAROLINA.
[MARC TREIB, 1980]

metamorphose into meaning over time. But to these must be added the memories triggered by the built world that stimulates accumulation or recall.

Thus, whether intended or not, architecture and designed landscapes serve as grand mnemonic devices that record and transmit vital aspects of culture and history. Cemeteries and memorials are types of built environments that pursue meaning as part of their making, purposefully. Houses and gymnasia do so, perhaps, to a lesser degree— although one can never dismiss the semantic aspects of design and construction even if not consciously cast as a part of their design. These all represent new constructions that engage with the past, and what has passed far outweighs what is present. As Friedrich Nietzsche cautioned us: "Let us beware of saying that death is opposed to life. The living is merely a type of what is dead, and a very rare type" at that. To some degree we are controlled by the dead as we live with their achievements and residue in our traditions, our laws, our cities, and our buildings—an assertion fully explored by Robert Harrison in his book *The Dominion of the Dead*.[2]

Architects and landscape architects have addressed this idea of externalized memory in differing ways at different times, varying from the "emulation" characteristic of classicism to its nearly complete repudiation by modernist practice. Over the last decades the gradient between these two poles has fluctuated once again, bringing us memory-laden projects such as New Urbanism, postmodern historicism, site remediation, activist historic preservation, ecological re-creation, and our current malaise: an abstracted architecture seemingly conceived free of the considerations of site, program, and at times people —an attitude whose influence and dissemination would put the modernists to shame.

The subjects about which our contributors have written cast a broad net over the idea of memory. Although, as I noted above, not all construction engages actively with memory as its principal charge, one might argue that it must always engage it to some degree, even if passively. It has been said, for example, that every new work of art throws into a new perspective all those works that have preceded it, and that those precedents have, in fact, provided the opening and the context for the new work. (George Kubler's condensed study *The Shape of Time* masterfully examines this idea in relation to art and material culture).[3] In that sense memory needs to be understood as the trace of all that has gone before, whether it exists today as a tangible remain or as a vague yet lingering mental presence.

I must admit that in commissioning the lectures for our original symposium, and their revised and expanded form as essays in this book, I have used the word memory in a very broad and imprecise way, and my usage is certainly open to challenge. In some of the contributions a reader could justifiably claim that "history" or "culture" or "civilization" would more accurately apply than the word "memory". Yet at some level—however deeply buried within the structure or the landscape—I suspect that the trace of memory always lies behind history, culture, and civilization, and that perhaps that whisper of the past validates my use of the word.

This book derives from the symposium "Spatial Recall: The Place of Memory in Architecture and Landscape," held at the University of California, Berkeley, in March 2007. The program drew on both scholars and practicing designers and artists, attempting to provoke and balance a variety of perspectives on the subject of memory. The presentations ranged from broad topics of message and audience to more specific issues concerning the production of design. Some addressed cities as a whole, others buildings taken as fragments. One talk focused on "nature's memory" as represented by the form and flow of rivers; others confronted nature's memory in new designs.

A recurring theme in many of the essays addresses the inter-relation of personal and collective memory. The paintings by Franco Magnani, discussed in the second chapter, demonstrate how vividly the mind can grasp images of house and village even after 30 years have passed. But is anything truly personal or truly collective, or is there always some transaction between the two domains? Does not the collective represent the summation of personal recall, or parts of that recall that are more social and group in nature rather than individual and idiosyncratic? Does not the collective memory require a personal experience and interpretation, as argued in the concluding chapter of the book in relation to historic preservation?

Other authors suggest that the manner in which a building is designed can engage people in ways that stimulate the collection of memories. Do certain architectural shapes and features, configurations and spaces, foster richer and longer-lasting memories?[4] And conversely, how do we look at the recollections embedded in existing built and natural environments as foundations for creating vibrant and significant new places? "We can not not know history," we are told.[5] Can we not not know memory? Memory haunts not only the derelict house but also the vibrant plaza. It haunts built worlds that have fallen to natural disasters or to changes of political regime.[6] In each case, the built form operates in a milieu propelled by memory although tempered by contemporary norms for living and building. How do we regard the past? As something to be banished and dismissed, or something to be actively engaged? The retention of ruins in contemporary park design raises a number of these questions, although it is but one design type.

Human memory is acquired; we are born with a clean slate upon which experience makes its marks. As with the human, so with the built environment. Most societies respect the aged as sources of a wisdom acquired through time and experience. Buildings and landscapes, too, can acquire wisdom in their fabrics. They can tell us things, should we choose to ask and listen—and of course, assuming we know their language. Alois Riegl proposed that one of the first characteristics of the monument worthy of preservation is its "age value".[7] Having existed for many years the structure has assumed an importance within the culture and presumably has things to tell. The structure or landscape may provoke memories, but its construction, use, and modification over time in themselves embodies memories then passed on to the next generation of visitors.[8] This process is a give and take between the environment, the individual, and society as a group. Thus, we might say that there are both memories in and memories (projected) upon our built environment—they become repositories into which, and from which—like a bank—both deposits and withdrawals may be transacted: the built environment as a memory bank, both individual and communal.

It is obvious that the subject of memory in architecture and landscape architecture possesses dimensions and a scale

[0–2]

DWELLING BUILT INTO CHURCH STRUCTURE, NORMANDY, FRANCE.
[MARC TREIB, 1975]

that can hardly be covered in a single volume. Like memory itself, the study of memory resembles an onion with its countless layers to be peeled away in search of its core. Yet despite these limitations I hope that the range and quality of these chapters will stimulate and inform the reader, as well as lay a firm foundation upon which can be built the ideas that will expand our knowledge of the subject.

Marc Treib
Berkeley
August 2008

NOTES

1 Frances Yates, *The Art of Memory*, Chicago: University of Chicago Press, 1966.

2 Robert Harrison, *The Dominion of the Dead*, Chicago: University of Chicago Press, 2003.

3 George Kubler, *The Shape of Time*, New Haven: Yale University Press, 1962.

4 For example, Levi Smith attributes much of the power of the Vietnam Memorial in Washington, D.C. to its reflective surface. "Window or Mirror: The Vietnam Veterans Memorial and the Ambiguity of Remembrance," in Peter Homans, ed., *Symbolic Loss: The Ambiguity of Mourning and Memory at Century's End*, Charlottesville: University of Virginia Press, 2000, pp. 105–125.

5 The source of the quote is Philip Johnson. See Kazys Varnelis, "Philip Johnson's Politics and Cynical Survival," *Journal of Architectural Education*, November 1994. Online version: http:// varnelis.net/articles/we_cannot_not_know_history, accessed 1 December 2008.

6 On destruction by war and purposeful demolition see Robert Bevin, *The Destruction of Memory: Architecture at War*, London: Reaktion, 2006.

7 Alois Riegl, "The Modern Cult of Monuments: Its Character and Its Origin," 1903, trans. Kurt W. Forster and Diane Ghirardo, *Oppositions* 25 (Fall 1982), pp. 21–51.

8 For a discussion of re-use and the transformation of intended meaning, see Jas Elsner, "Iconoclasm and the Preservation of Memory," in Robert S. Nelson and Margaret Olin, eds, *Monuments and Memory, Made and Unmade*, Chicago: University of Chicago Press, 2003, pp. 209–231.

[1]
Space, Place, Memory, and Imagination: The Temporal Dimension of Existential Space

Juhani Pallasmaa

Architecture is usually seen in futuristic terms: novel buildings are understood to probe and project an unforeseen reality, and architectural quality is directly associated with its degree of novelty and uniqueness. Modernity at large has been dominated by this futuristic bias. Yet the appreciation of newness has probably never been as obsessive as in today's cult of spectacular architectural imagery. In our globalized world, newness is not only an aesthetic and artistic value, it is a strategic necessity of the culture of consumption and, consequently, an inseparable ingredient of our surreal materialist culture.

However, human constructions also have the task of preserving the past, enabling us to experience and grasp the continuum of culture and tradition. We do not only exist in a spatial and material reality, we also inhabit cultural, mental, and temporal realities. Our existential and lived reality is a thick, layered, and constantly oscillating condition. Architecture is essentially an art form of reconciliation and mediation and in addition to settling us in space and place, landscapes and buildings articulate our experiences of duration and time between the polarities of past and future. In fact, along with the entire corpus of literature and the arts, landscapes and buildings constitute the most important externalization of human memory. We understand and remember who we are through our constructions, both material and mental. We also judge alien and past cultures through the evidence provided by the architectural structures they have produced. Buildings project epic narratives.

In addition to practical purposes, architectural structures have a significant existential and mental task; they domesticate space for human occupation by turning anonymous, uniform, and limitless space into distinct places of human significance, and equally importantly they make endless time tolerable by giving duration its human measure. As the philosopher Karsten Harries argues,

> Architecture helps to replace meaningless reality with a theatrically, or rather architecturally, transformed reality, which draws us in and, as we surrender to it, grants us an illusion of meaning ... we cannot live with chaos. Chaos must be transformed into cosmos.[1]

[1–1]
ABANDONED GARAGE,
PIETOWN, NEW MEXICO.
[MARC TREIB]

He states in another context, "Architecture is not only about domesticating space. [I]t is also a deep defence against the terror of time."[2] Altogether, environments and buildings do not only serve practical and utilitarian purposes; they also structure our understanding of the world. "[The house] is an instrument with which to confront the cosmos," as Gaston Bachelard notes.[3] The abstract and indefinable notion of cosmos is always present and represented in our immediate landscape. Every landscape and every building is a condensed world, a microcosmic representation.

ARCHITECTURE AND MEMORY

We all remember the way architectural images were utilized as mnemonic devices by the orators of antiquity. Built structures, as well as mere remembered architectural images and meta-phors, serve as significant memory devices in three different ways: first, they materialize and preserve the course of time and make it visible; second, they concretize remembrance by containing and projecting memories; and third, they stimulate and inspire us to reminisce and imagine [1–1]. Memory and fantasy, recollection and imagination, are related and they have always a situational and specific content. One who can-not remember can hardly imagine because memory is the soil of the imagination. Memory is also the ground of self-identity; we are what we remember.

Buildings are storage houses and museums of time and silence. Architectural structures have the capacity of trans-forming, speeding up, slowing down, and halting time. They can also create and protect silence following Kierkegaard's request: "Create silence!"[4] In the view of Max Picard, the philosopher of silence, "Nothing has changed the nature of man so much as the loss of silence."[5] "Silence no longer exists as a world, but only in fragments, as the remains of a world."[6] Architecture has to preserve the memory of the world of silence and to protect the existing fragments of this fundamental ontological state. As we enter a Romanesque monastery we can still experience the benevolent silence of the universe.

There are, of course, particular building types—such as memorials, tombs, and museums—that are deliberately conceived and built for the purpose of preserving and evoking memories and specific emotions. Buildings can maintain feelings of grief and ecstasy, melancholy and joy, as well as fear and hope. All buildings maintain our perception of temporal duration and depth, and they record and suggest cultural and human narratives. We cannot conceive or remember time as a mere physical dimension; we can only grasp time through its actualizations: the traces, places, and events of temporal occurrence. Joseph Brodsky points out another deficiency of human memory as he writes about the composite images of cities in human memory and finds these cities always empty: "[The city of memory] is empty because for an imagination it is easier to conjure architecture than human beings."[7] Is this the inherent reason why we architects tend to think of architecture more in terms of its material existence than the life and human situations that take place in the spaces we have designed?

Architectural structures facilitate memory; our understanding of the depth of time would be decisively weaker, for instance, without the image of the pyramids in our minds. The mere image of a pyramid marks and concretizes time. We also remember our own childhood largely through the houses and places that we have lived in. We have projected and hidden parts of our lives in lived landscapes and houses, exactly as the orators placed themes of their speeches in the context of imagined buildings. The recollection of places and rooms generates the recall of events and people. After having crash-landed with his plane in a sand desert in North Africa, Antoine de Saint-Exupéry, the legendary pilot and writer, reminisced:

> I was a child of that house, filled with the memory of its smells, filled with the coolness of its hallways, filled with the voices that had given it life. There was even the song of the frogs in the pools; they came to be with me here.[8]

THE MENTAL POWER OF FRAGMENTS

In his novel *The Notebooks of Malte Laurids Brigge*, Rainer Maria Rilke gives a similarly moving record of a distant memory of home and self arising from fragments of the grandfather's house in the protagonist's memory:

> As I recover it in recalling my child-wrought memories, it is no complete building: it is all broken up inside me; here a room, there a room, and here a piece of hallway that does not connect these two rooms but is preserved, as a fragment, by itself. In this way it is all dispersed within me ...all that is still in me and will never cease to be in me. It is as though the picture of this house had fallen into me from an infinite height and had shattered against my very ground.[9]

The remembered image arises gradually, piece by piece, from fragments of memory as a painted cubist picture emerges from detached visual motifs.

I have written about my own memories of my grandfather's humble farmhouse, and pointed out that the memory house of my early childhood is a collage of fragments, smells, conditions of light, and specific feelings of enclosure and intimacy, but rarely precise and complete visual recollections.[10]

My eyes have forgotten what they once saw, but my body still remembers. We internalize our experiences as lived situational, multi-sensory images and they are fused with our body experience. Human memory is embodied, skeletal and muscular in its essence, not merely cerebral.

Buildings and their remains suggest stories of human fate, both real and imaginary. Ruins stimulate us to think of lives that have already disappeared and to imagine the fate of their deceased occupants. Ruins and eroded settings have an especially evocative and emotional power; they force us to reminisce and imagine. Incompleteness and fragmentation possess a special evocative power. In medieval illustrations and Renaissance paintings architectural settings are often depicted as a mere edge of a wall or a window opening, but the isolated fragment suffices to conjure up the experience of a complete constructed setting. This is the secret of the art of collage but also architects such as John Soane and Alvar Aalto have taken advantage of this emotional power of the architectural fragment. Soane's own house at 13 Lincoln's Inn Fields in London (1792–1824) is a collection of architectural fragments and a constructed ruin, whereas the design strategy of Alvar Aalto's mature work is often based on the idea of an episodic collage of architectural events, images, and fragments [1–2, 1–3]. Rilke's description of the images of life lived in a demolished house, triggered by the remains and stains left on the end wall of the neighboring house, is a stunning record of the ways of human memory:

> But most forgettable of all were the walls themselves. The stubborn life of these rooms had not let itself be trampled out. It was still there; it clung to the nails that had been left there, it stood on the remaining hand-breadth of flooring, it crouched under the corner joints where there was

still a little bit of interior. One could see that it was in the paint which, year by year, had slowly altered: blue into moldy green, green into grey, and yellow into an old, stale rotting white.[11]

SPATIALITY AND SITUATIONALITY OF MEMORY

Our recollections are situational and spatialized memories; they are memories attached to places and events. It is hard to recall, for instance, a familiar or iconic photograph as a two-dimensional image on photographic paper; we tend to remember the depicted object, person, or event in its full spatial reality. It is obvious that our existential space is never a two-dimensional pictorial space, but a lived and multi-sensory space saturated and structured by memories and intentions. We keep projecting meanings and signification to everything we encounter. I have rarely disagreed with the views of Joseph Brodsky, one of my house gods, but when he argues that after having seen touristic buildings such as Westminster Abbey, the Eiffel Tower, St. Basil's, the Taj Mahal, or the Acropolis,

[1-2]
JOHN SOANE, SOANE HOUSE AND MUSEUM, LONDON, 1792–1834. STATUES AND ARCHITECTURAL FRAGMENTS. [MARC TREIB]

"we retain not their three-dimensional image but their printed version [1–4]." He concludes that: "Strictly speaking, we remember not a place but our postcard of it."[12] Here I must disagree with the poet. We do not remember the postcard but the real place pictured in it. A recalled image is always more than the once-seen image itself. In my view, Brodsky presents a rushed argument here, perhaps misguided by Susan Sontag's ideas of the power of the photographed image in her seminal book *On Photography*.[13]

Pictures, objects, fragments, and insignificant things, all serve as condensation centers for our memories. Jarkko Laine, the Finnish poet, writes about the role of objects in his memory:

> I like looking at these things. I don't seek aesthetic pleasure in them...nor do I recall their origins: that is not important. But even so they all arouse memories, real and imagined. A poem is a thing that arouses memories of real and imagined things...The things in the window act like a poem. They are images that do not reflect anything... I sing of the things in the window.[14]

[1–3]
ALVAR AALTO,
EXPERIMENTAL HOUSE,
MUURATSALO,
FINLAND, 1954.
WALL DETAIL.
[MARC TREIB]

The significance of objects in our processes of remembering is the main reason why we like to collect familiar or peculiar objects around us; they expand and reinforce the realm of memories, and eventually, our very sense of self. Few of the objects we possess are really needed strictly for utilitarian purposes: their function is social and mental as well. "I am what is around me," argues Wallace Stevens, whereas Nöel Arnaud, another poet, claims: "I am the space, where I am."[15] These condensed formulations by two poets emphasize the intertwining of the world and the self as well as the externalized ground of remembrance and identity.

A room can also be individualized and taken into one's possession by turning it into a place of dreaming; the acts of memorizing and dreaming are interrelated. As Bachelard puts it: "[T]he house shelters daydreaming, the house protects the dreamer, the house allows one to dream in peace."[16] A fundamental quality of a landscape, house, and room is its capacity to evoke and contain a feeling of safety, familiarity, at-homeness, and to stimulate fantasies. We are not capable of deep imagination outdoors in wild nature; profound imagination calls for the focusing intimacy of a room. For me, the real measure of the quality of a town is whether I can imagine myself falling in love there.

THE LIVED WORLD

We do not live in an objective world of matter and fact, as commonplace naive realism tends to assume. The characteristically human mode of existence takes place in the worlds of possibilities, molded by the human capacity of remembrance, fantasy, and imagination. We live in mental worlds in which the material and the spiritual, as well as the experienced, the remembered, and the imagined, constantly fuse into each other.

[1–4]
KALLIKRATES AND
PHEIDIAS, PARTHENON,
ATHENS, 438 BCE.
[MARC TREIB]

As a consequence, the lived reality does not follow the rules of space and time as defined and measured by the science of physics. I wish to argue that the lived world is fundamentally "unscientific," when measured by the criteria of Western empirical science. In fact, the lived world is closer to the reality of dream than any scientific description. To distinguish the lived space from physical and geometrical space, we can call it "existential space." Lived existential space is structured on the basis of meanings, intentions, and values reflected upon it by an individual, either consciously or unconsciously; existential space is a unique quality interpreted through the memory and experience of the individual. Every lived experience takes place at the interface of recollection and intention, perception and fantasy, memory and desire. T. S. Eliot brings forth the important pairing of opposites at the end of his fourth quartet, "Little Gidding":

> What we call the beginning is often the end. And to make an end is to make a beginning. ... We shall not cease from exploration. And the end of all our exploring will be to arrive where we started. And know the place for the first time.[17]

On the other hand, collective groups—or even nations —share certain experiences of existential space that constitute their collective identities and sense of togetherness. We are, perhaps, held together by our shared memories more than by an innate sense of solidarity. I wish to recall here the sociological study by Maurice Halbwachs which revealed that the ease of mutual communication between old Parisians living within a distinct quarter was grounded in their rich and shared collective memories [1–5].

The lived space is also the object and context of both the making and experiencing of art as well as architecture. Art projects a lived reality, not mere symbolic representations of life.

The task of architecture is, as well, "to make visible how the world touches us," as Merleau-Ponty wrote of the paintings of Paul Cezanne.[18] We live in the "flesh of the world," to use a notion of the philosopher, and landscapes and architecture structure and articulate this existential flesh, giving it specific horizons and meanings.

EXPERIENCE AS EXCHANGE

Remembering is not only a mental event; it is also an act of embodiment and projection. Memories are not only hidden in the secret electrochemical processes of the brain; they are also stored in our skeletons, muscles, and skin. All our senses and organs think and remember.

The experience of a place or space is always a curious exchange; as I settle in a space, the space settles in me. I live in a city and the city dwells in me. We are in a constant exchange with our settings; simultaneously we internalize the setting and project our own bodies, or aspects of our bodily schemes, upon the setting. Memory and actuality, perception and dream, merge. This secret physical and mental intertwining and identification also takes place in all artistic experience. In Joseph Brodsky's view, every poem tells the reader "Be like me."[19] Here lies the ethical power of all authentic works of art; we internalize them and integrate them with our very sense of self. A fine piece of music, poetry, or architecture becomes a part of my physical and moral self. The Czech writer Bohumil Hrabal gives a vivid description of this bodily association in the act of reading:

[1–5]
SITTING ON BENCHES,
VILLANDRY, FRANCE.
[MARC TREIB, 2005]

When I read, I don't really read; I pop a beautiful sentence
in my mouth and suck it like a fruit drop or I sip it like
a liqueur until the thought dissolves in me like alcohol,
infusing my brain and heart and coursing on through the
veins to the root of each blood vessel.[20]

THE EMBODIED MEMORY

I can recall the hundreds of hotel rooms around the world
which I have temporarily inhabited during my five decades of
travelling—with their furniture, color schemes, and lighting
—because I have invested and left parts of my body and my
mind in these anonymous and insignificant rooms [1–6]. The
protagonist of Marcel Proust's *In Search of Lost Time* recon-
structs similarly his very identity and location through his
embodied memory:

My body, still too heavy with sleep to move, would endeav-
our to construe from the pattern of its tiredness the position
of its various limbs, in order to deduce therefrom the
direction of the wall, the location of the furniture, to piece
together and give a name to the house in which it lay. Its
memory, the composite memory of its ribs, its knees, its
shoulder-blades, offered it a whole series of rooms in which
it had at one time or another slept, while the unseen walls,
shifting and adapting themselves to the shape of each
successive room that it remembered, whirled it in the dark
... my body, would recall from each room in succession
the style of the bed, the position of the doors, the angle at
which the sunlight came in at the windows, whether there
was a passage outside, what I had had in mind when I
went to sleep and found there when I awoke.[21]

We are again encountering an experience that brings to mind
a fragmented Cubist composition. We are taught to think of
memory as a cerebral capacity, but the act of memory engages
our entire body.

[1–6]
WINDOW WITH
PLASTIC CURTAINS,
AMBOISE, FRANCE.
[MARC TREIB, 1988]

"[B]ody memory is … the natural center of any sensitive account of remembering," the philosopher Edward S. Casey argues in his seminal book *Memorizing: A Phenomenological Study,* and concludes: "There is no memory without body memory."[22] In my view we could say even more: the body is not only the locus of remembrance, it is also the site and medium of all creative work, including the work of the architect.

[1–7]
MICHELANGELO,
MEDICI TOMB,
NEW SACRISTY,
SAN LORENZO,
FLORENCE, 1520–1524;
1530–1533.
[MARC TREIB]

MEMORY AND EMOTION

In addition to being memory devices, landscapes and buildings are also amplifiers of emotions; they reinforce sensations of belonging or alienation, invitation or rejection, tranquillity or despair. A landscape or work of architecture cannot, however, create feelings. Through their authority and aura, they evoke and strengthen our own emotions and project them back to us as if these feelings of ours had an external source [1–7]. In the Laurentian Library in Florence I confront my own sense of metaphysical melancholy awakened and projected back by

Michelangelo's architecture. The strange positioning and proportioning of the columns and volutes conveys the hallucinating architectural experience of being under water giving rise to an altered state of consciousness. The optimism experienced when approaching the Paimio Sanatorium is the sense of hope evoked and strengthened by Alvar Aalto's optimistic architecture [1–8]. The white purity and vitality of the architectural language projects a sense of optimism and healing. The hill of the meditation grove at the Woodland Cemetery outside Stockholm, for instance, evokes a state of longing and hope through an image that is an invitation and a promise [1–9]. This architectural image of landscape evokes simultaneously remembrance and imagination as the composite painted image of Arnold Böcklin's *Island of the Dead*. All poetic images are condensations of imagery and memory and microcosmic representations of the world.

"House, even more than the landscape, is a psychic state," Bachelard suggests.[23] Indeed, writers, film directors, poets, and painters do not just depict landscapes or houses as the unavoidable geographic and physical settings of the events of their stories; they seek to express, evoke, and amplify human emotions, mental states, and memories through purposeful depictions of settings, both natural and man-made. "Let us assume a wall: what takes place behind it?" asks the poet Jean Tardieu, but we architects rarely bother to imagine what takes place behind the walls we have erected.[24] The walls conceived by architects are usually mere aestheticized constructions, and we see our craft in terms of designing aesthetic structures rather than evoking perceptions, feelings, and fantasies.

Artists seem to grasp the intertwining of place and human mind, memory and desire, much better than we architects do, and that is why these other art forms can provide such stimulating inspiration for our work as well as for architectural education. There are no better lessons of the extraordinary capacity of artistic condensations in evoking microcosmic images of the world than, say, the short stories of Anton Chekhov and Jorge Luis Borges, or Giorgio Morandi's minute still-lifes consisting of only a few bottles and cups set on a table top.

SLOWNESS AND REMEMBERING; SPEED AND FORGETTING

"There is a secret bond between slowness and memory, between speed and forgetting…the degree of slowness is directly proportional to the intensity of memory: the degree of speed is directly proportional to the intensity of forgetting." So suggests the Czech novelist Milan Kundera.[25] With the dizzying acceleration of the velocity of time today and the constant speeding up of our experiential reality, we are seriously threatened by a general cultural amnesia. In today's accelerated life we can ultimately only perceive, not remember. In

[1–9]
GUNNAR ASPLUND AND
SIGURD LEWERENTZ,
WOODLAND CEMETERY,
ENSKEDE, SWEDEN,
1940.
MEDITATION KNOLL.
[MARC TREIB]

the society of the spectacle we can only marvel, not remember. We may not be aware of this shallowing of memory in our own daily lives, but the flattening of human memory becomes evident when comparing the density of observations in nineteenth- and early-twentieth-century classical literature with today's typical literary narration: "the flattest possible characters in the flattest possible landscapes rendered in the flattest possible diction," as Charles Newman describes the New American Novel.[26] Speed and transparency weaken remembrance but they have been fundamental fascinations of Modernity since the proclamation of F. T. Marinetti in the *Futurist Manifesto* almost a full century ago: "The world's magnificence has been enriched by a new beauty; the beauty of speed."[27] Add to that Karl Marx's prophesy: "Everything that is solid...melts into the air."[28] Today, even architecture seeks the sensation of speed, instant seduction, and gratification, and as a consequence turns autistic. The confession of Coop Himmelb(l)au illustrates this aspiration for dramatized architectural action and speed:

> The aesthetics of the architecture of death in white sheets. Death in tiled hospital rooms. The architecture of sudden death on the pavement. Death from a rib-cage pierced by a steering shaft. The path of the bullet through a dealer's head on 42nd Street. The aesthetics of the peep-show sex in washable plastic boxes. Of the broken tongues and the dried-up eyes.[29]

In my view, however, architecture is inherently a slow and quiet, emotionally low-energy art form in comparison with the dramatic arts of sudden affective impact. Its role is not to create strong foreground figures or feelings but to establish frames of perception and horizons of understanding. The task of architecture is not to make us weep or laugh but to sensitize us to be able to enter all emotional states. Architecture is needed to provide the ground and projection screen of remembrance and emotion.

I believe in an architecture that slows down and focuses human experience instead of diffusing or speeding it up. In my view, architecture has to safeguard memories and protect the authenticity and independence of human experience. Architecture is fundamentally the art form of emancipation that makes us understand and remember who we are.

ARCHITECTURAL AMNESIA

There are different kinds of architecture in relation to memory: one that cannot recall or touch upon the past, and another that evokes a sense of depth and continuity. There is also an architecture that seeks to remember literally, like the architectural works of historicist postmodernism, and another that creates a sense of deep time and epic continuity without any direct formal reference—such as the works of Alvar Aalto, Dimitris Pikionis, and Carlo Scarpa [1–10, 1–11]. This is an architecture that evokes a primordial, unspecified awareness of the past and temporal duration, and a layered sense of time. Its emotive and associative power lies in the total fusion of ingredients into an indivisible entity. These are products of a "poetic chemistry," to use an evocative notion of Bachelard.[30] Every significant and true work sets itself in a respectful dialog with the past, both distant and immediate. At the same time that the work defends itself as a unique and complete microcosm, it revives and revitalizes the past. Every true work of art occupies a thick and layered time instead of mere contemporaneity.

There is yet another dimension in architectural memory. Architectural images and experiences have a historicity and

ontology of their own. Architecture begins with the establish-
ment of a horizontal plane; consequently, the floor is the
"oldest" and most potent element of architecture. The wall
is more archaic than the door or the window and as a consequence it projects a deeper meaning. Modernity has suffered
from another kind of amnesia as architectural elements and
images have become abstracted and detached from their origins
and ontological essences. The experientially and phenomeno-
logically oriented study of architecture aims at recovering and
re-memorizing the ontological essence of fundamental and
primary architectural experiences, such as the "floorness" of the
floor, the "roofness" of the roof, and the mental essences of the
door and the window. The floor, for instance, has forgotten
its origin as levelled earth, and turned into mere constructed
horizontal planes. In fact, as Bachelard suggests, human constructions of the technological age have forgotten verticality
altogether and turned into mere horizontality. Today's skyscrapers consist of stacked horizontalities and have lost the
sense of verticality, the fundamental ontological difference
between above and below, heaven and hell. We can still
experience height and vertigo but the metaphysical meaning
and experiential excitement of the vertical ascent of the towers
and cathedrals of history, as well as of early modern skyscrapers,

[1–10] *above*
DIMITRIS PIKIONIS,
ROADWORK,
FILOPÁPPOS HILL,
ATHENS, 1954–1957.
[MARC TREIB]

[1–11] *opposite*
CARLO SCARPA,
PALAZZO QUERINI-
STAMPAGLIA,
VENICE, 1963.
INTERIOR STEPS
FROM THE LOBBY TO
THE CANAL.
[MARC TREIB]

is lost. In addition, the floor and the ceiling have become identical horizontal planes. The window and the door are often mere holes in the wall. I do not have the space here to elaborate on this theme of the historicity of architectural images and the current architectural amnesia resulting from the loss of the historicity of experiences; I merely point at the mental significance of this dimension.

THE TENSES OF ART

I venture to suggest that in its very essence artistic work is oriented towards the past rather than the future. Brodsky seems to support this view as he argues: "There is something clearly atavistic in the process of recollection, if only because such a process never is linear. Also the more one remembers, the closer perhaps one is to dying."[31]

In any significant experience, temporal layers interact; what is perceived interacts with what is remembered, the novel short-circuits with the archaic. An artistic experience always awakens the forgotten child hidden inside one's adult persona.

There are fabricated images in today's architecture and art that are flat and without an emotional echo, but there are also novel images that resonate with remembrance. The latter are at the same time mysterious and familiar, obscure and clear. They move us through the remembrances and associations, emotions and empathy that they awaken in us. Artistic novelty can move us only provided it touches something that we already possess in our very being. Every profound artistic work surely grows from memory, not from rootless intellectual invention. Artistic works aspire to bring us back to an undivided and undifferentiated oceanic world. This is the Omega that Teilhard de Chardin writes about, "the point from which the world appears complete and correct."[32]

We are usually conditioned to think that artists and architects ought to be addressing the future readers, viewers, and users of their products. Joseph Brodsky is very determined, indeed, about the poet's temporal perspective: "When one writes, one's most immediate audience is not one's own contemporaries, let alone posterity, but one's predecessors."[33] "No real writer ever wanted to be contemporary," Jorge Luis Borges argues in the same vein.[34] This view opens another essential perspective on the significance and role of remembrance; all creative work is collaboration with the past and with the wisdom of tradition. Milan Kundera suggests that:

> Every true novelist listens for that suprapersonal wisdom [the wisdom of the novel], which explains why great novels are always a little more intelligent than their authors. Novelists who are more intelligent than their books should go into another line of work.[35]

The same observation is equally true of architecture; great buildings are fruits of the wisdom of architecture, they are products of a collaboration, often unconscious, with our great predecessors as much as they are works of their individual creators. Only works that are in vital and respectful dialog with their past possess the mental capacity to survive time and stimulate viewers, listeners, readers, and occupants in the future.

NOTES

1 Karsten Harries, "Thoughts on a Non-Arbitrary Architecture," in David Seamon, ed., *Dwelling, Seeing, and Designing: Toward a Phenomenological Ecology*, Albany: State University of New York Press, 1993, p. 47.

2 Karsten Harries, "Building and the Terror of Time," *Perspecta: The Yale Architectural Journal*, 19, Cambridge: MIT Press, 1982. Quoted in David Harvey, *The Condition of Post-modernity*, Cambridge: Blackwell, 1992, p. 206.

3 Gaston Bachelard, *The Poetics of Space*, Boston: Beacon Press, 1969, p. 46.

4 Quoted in Max Picard, *The World of Silence*, Washington, D.C.: Regnery Gateway, 1988, p. 231. Kierkegaard writes: "The present state of the world and the whole of life is dis-eased. If I were a doctor and were asked for my advice, I should say: Create Silence! Bring men to silence."

5 Ibid., p. 221.

6 Ibid., p. 212.

7 Joseph Brodsky, "A Place as Good as Any," in *On Grief and Reason*, New York: Farrar, Straus and Giroux, 1997, p. 43.

8 Antoine de Saint-Exupéry, *Wind, Sand and Stars*, London: Penguin Books, 1991, p. 39.

9 Rainer Maria Rilke, *The Notebooks of Malte Laurids Brigge*, trans. M. O. Herter Norton, New York and London: W.W. Norton, 1992, pp. 30–31.

10 Juhani Pallasmaa, "The Geometry of Feeling: The Phenomenology of Architecture" (1985), in Juhani Pallasmaa: *Encounters*, Peter MacKeith, ed., Helsinki: Rakennustieto Oy, 2005, pp. 86–97.

11 Rilke, *Notebooks*, pp. 47–48.

12 Brodsky, "A Place as Good as Any," p. 37.

13 Susan Sontag, *On Photography*, Harmondworth, England: Penguin Books, 1986.

14 Jarkko Laine, "Tikusta asiaa," *Parnasso* 6:1982, pp. 323–324.

15 Wallace Stevens, "Theory," in *The Collected Poems*, New York: Vintage Books, 1990, p. 86; Noël Arnaud, quoted in Bachelard, *Poetics of Space*, p. 137.

16 Bachelard, *Poetics of Space*, p. 6.

17 T. S. Eliot, *Four Quartets*, New York: Harcourt Brace Jovanovich Publishers, 1971, pp. 58; 59.

18 Maurice Merleau-Ponty, "Cezanne's Doubt," in *Sense and Non-Sense*, Evanston, IL: Northwestern University Press, 1964, p. 19.

19 Brodsky, *On Grief and Reason*, p. 206.

20 Bohumil Hrabal, *Too Loud a Solitude*, New York: Harcourt, Inc., 1990, p. 1.

21 Marcel Proust, *In Search of Lost Time: Swann's Way*, trans. C. K. Scott Moncrieff and Terence Kilmartin, London: Random House, 1992, pp. 4–5.

22 Edward S. Casey, *Memorizing: A Phenomenological Study*, Bloomington, IL: Indiana University Press, 2000, pp. 148; 172.

23 Bachelard, *Poetics of Space*, p. 72.

24 Quoted in Georges Perec, *Tiloja ja avaruuksia [Espéces d'espaces]*, Helsinki: Loki-Kirjat, 1992, p. 72.

25 Milan Kundera, *Slowness*, New York: HarperCollins, 1966, p. 39.

26 Charles Newman, *New York Times*, 17 July 1987, quoted in David Harvey, *The Condition of Postmodernity*, Cambridge, Mass.: Blackwell Publishers, 1992, p. 58.

27 Quoted in: Thom Mayne, "Statement," *Peter Pran*, Ligang Qui, ed., China: DUT Press, 2006, p. 4.

28 "All fixed, fast-frozen relations, with their train of ancient and venerable prejudices and opinions, are swept away, all newformed ones become antiquated before they can ossify. All that is solid melts into air, all that is holy is profaned, and men at last are forced to face … the real conditions of their lives and their relations with their fellow men." Karl Marx, *Communist Manifesto*, 1848, quoted in Marshall Berman, *All That Is Solid Melts Into Air: The Experience of Modernity*, London and New York: Verso, 1990, p. 21.

29 Coop Himmelblau, "Die Fascination der Stadt," quoted in Anthony Vidler, *The Architectural Uncanny*, Cambridge, Mass.: MIT Press, 1999, p. 76.

30 Gaston Bachelard, *Water and Dreams: An Essay on the Imagination of Matter*, Dallas, TX: The Pegasus Foundation, 1983, p. 46.

31 Joseph Brodsky, "Less Than One," in Joseph Brodsky, *Less Than One*, New York: Farrar, Straus Giroux, 1998, p. 30.

32 Quoted in Timo Valjakka, ed., *Juhana Blomstedt: Muodon arvo*, Helsinki: Painatuskeskus, 1995, p. 94.

33 Joseph Brodsky, "Letter to Horace," in *On Grief and Reason*, p. 439.

34 *Borges on Writing*, eds., Norman Thomas di Giovanni, Daniel Halpern, and Frank MacShane, Hopewell, NJ: Ecco Press, 1994, p. 53.

35 Milan Kundera, *The Art of the Novel*, New York: HarperCollins, 2000, p. 158.

[2]
Re-creating
the Past:
Notes on
the Neurology
of Memory

Susan Schwartzenberg

The Exploratorium in San Francisco is a museum of science, art, and human perception. As an institution the museum believes that both artists and scientists provide insight into understanding the world and its mandate ensures that art and science equally inform the development of exhibits, programs, and teaching strategies. All the exhibits are designed, prototyped, tested, and built on site with the intention of providing direct access to scientific phenomena through interactive engagement.

Over the years since the Exploratorium's founding in 1969 its exhibits have evolved from those addressing human perception (eye physiology, optics, illusions) to those more concerned with cognition (language, memory, mind, seeing, and listening).[1] As part of the museum's Mind series, for example, a recent exhibit involved the conversion of a toilet into a drinking fountain. In this exhibit—titled "A Sip of Conflict"—visitors were assured that the toilet has never been used for sanitary functions; nonetheless, no one would use it for drinking. This cognitive censorship suggests the power of memory in creating the context for meaning that surrounds any object or place—attitudes often very difficult to break. Exhibits such as these shift the focus from the object to the visitor, attempting to discover ways for people to become cognizant of how their minds work, what they pay attention to, and ultimately how they make decisions. As a Senior Artist at the Exploratorium my role is to ensure that we balance art and science when developing our exhibits and programs.

A MEMORY ARTIST

The shift in emphasis from perception to cognition began in 1987 when Bob Miller, a senior staff artist at the Exploratorium, introduced me to the story of his friend Franco Magnani. In 1965 Magnani had emigrated from Italy and settled in San Francisco's North Beach district. Some years later, from memory, he began painting images of his natal village. Born in 1934, Franco had grown up in Pontito, a small Italian town north of Florence. After World War II, like many young adults in that region, he left home in search of work in a post-war economy no longer able to support the cottage and collective industries that had once thrived in these rural villages. Although trained as a cabinetmaker, Franco crossed the ocean as a chef on a cruise liner. After a stressful period working in the

[2-1A] *left*
FRANCO MAGNANI, VIEW FROM FRANCO'S ROOM, PONTITO, ITALY, c.1984. OIL ON CANVAS BOARD.

[2-1B] *right*
SUSAN SCHWARTZENBERG, VIEW FROM FRANCO'S ROOM, PONTITO, ITALY, 1987.
COLOR COUPLER PRINT.

TO RECORD THIS VIEW FRANCO HAD PAINTED OF HIS MEMORY OF HIS CHILDHOOD ROOM, I POSITIONED MYSELF AT VARIOUS POINTS IN THE ROOM AND SAW MUCH OF THE LANDSCAPE DEPICTED IN THE PAINTING —BUT THERE WAS NOWHERE IN THE ROOM WHERE I COULD STAND AND CAPTURE THE SAME SCENE IN THE PAINTING. HIS MEMORY IS BASED UPON LIVING IN THE ROOM AND SEEING THE LANDSCAPE FROM MULTIPLE VIEWS.

restaurant business in San Francisco—troubled by constant scares about immigration quotas—he fell ill with what was suspected of being tuberculosis. During his recuperation he began painting scenes of his hometown from memory. Although he had never returned to Pontito after his initial departure, he created an impressive, and somewhat compulsive, body of paintings and drawings executed in what appeared to be exacting detail. My assignment was to meet Franco, photograph his paintings, travel to Pontito, locate the scenes he depicted, and as closely as possible replicate their views in photographs. The paintings and photographs would provide the materials for an exhibition that would explore these relationships and suggest what we could learn about memory from them.[2]

At our first meeting I was overwhelmed by Franco. He spoke a very fast version of Italian/English and jumped from story to story—stories always about Pontito. He recounted the years of his childhood, his mother and sisters, the fields and houses, the war, Mussolini. He was highly animated as he spoke and seemed to be transported by his own recollections. I knew he was a self-taught or "naive" painter but I had not seen any of his work until then. My concern grew as his stream of incomprehensible stories appeared to have no end. Eventually, however, he unrolled the poster tucked under his arm, revealing a print of one of his paintings [2–1A, 2–1B]. The painting had a naive quality, but in manner it contrasted markedly with how Franco's personality seemed to me. It was well ordered, with a strong sense of longing, nostalgia, or homesickness. Within the room the painted colors were subdued, but the window framed a charming and harmonious view of a vibrant landscape beyond the building.

Much of my own work has explored ways to connect individual lives with collective histories. How do individuals

[2–2A] *left*
FRANCO MAGNANI, VIEW THROUGH THE CAMPANILE, c.1984. OIL ON CANVAS BOARD.

[2–2B] *right*
SUSAN SCHWARTZENBERG, VIEW THROUGH THE CAMPANILE, 1987. PHOTOGRAPH.

create meaningful existences around them? How do we construct a psychology of place for those spaces in which we live? After this one unusual meeting I was interested to learn how Franco had become separated, partly by choice, from this place of his past and why he now had returned to that town through hundreds of paintings and drawings. I saw this project as an opportunity to bring the story of the person into the broader study of perception and into a "museum of science." Over the next several months I photographed Franco's paintings and drawings until I had compiled a complete archive of his work.[3]

Franco's work is comprehensive and encyclopedic in the sense that sections of the village are viewed time and again from various directions. His paintings are mostly depopulated. The noted neurologist Oliver Sacks likened them to the metaphysical paintings of Giorgio de Chirico, although they are not nearly as ominous. Franco's efforts display a sensitivity to shadows, time of day, and seasonal light, but in every painting the shadows serve as a nostalgic device that seems to further idealize his sense of place [2–2A, 2–2B]. Each painting and drawing displays a similar sense of order, serenity, and longing.

When I left for Pontito I already believed in Franco's powerful ability to remember but I was also skeptical that his drawings and paintings were "photographic" or specifically and accurately detailed. I had come to realize there was a deeper story here: the story of immigration, the loss of the village community of his childhood, and the loss of his mother. Though Franco's mother had died in 1972 she had seen Franco's first painting in a snapshot he had sent her, and in a letter she told him how the image had brought her back to the family's pre-war life and times, when Franco's father still lived and the village was productive.

In Pontito I stayed with Franco's sister and her husband. On my first day there I showed them the notebook of Franco's paintings after which we made our first tour of the village. Evidently, people in the village were expecting me because they joined in discussing the locations of the various scenes [2–3]. As we walked from street to street, everyone engaged in our project to find the "real sites" depicted in Franco's paintings. That the village was on a very steep hill came as a surprise to me as it did not appear that way in the paintings. The village also seemed a lot smaller in reality than in the paintings— typical memory distortions I would later learn to decipher.

Returning to San Francisco after two weeks in Pontito I prepared a set of boards pairing the paintings with my own photographs. My colleagues and I stared at them for a while and then solicited opinions from a variety of scientists, asking them what the images might relate about memory and the process of remembering.

Before the war over one thousand people had lived in Pontito, collectively farming chestnuts and walnuts, individually tending their own vegetable gardens, and raising small fowl and rabbits. Their produce was supplemented by traveling to the markets of Pescha to purchase or trade for beef and fish. Most men found supplemental employment in the surrounding paper mills and munitions factories. In fact, Franco's father had died in a factory accident in 1942. The comparison between Franco's paintings and the photographs might suggest that he had idealized the scene, while in fact the images spoke of the remarkable historical changes that had occurred: for example, with few residents left to tend the fields the surrounding landscape had become overgrown [2–4]. Less than 90 people then lived in Pontito and almost all of them had returned only in their retirement. While remarkable in the basic accuracy of

[2-3] *left above*

SUSAN SCHWARTZENBERG,
VILLAGERS IN PONTITO
DISCUSSING THE VIEWS IN
FRANCO'S PAINTINGS.
PHOTOGRAPH.

[2-4] *left below*

SUSAN SCHWARTZENBERG,
CARRYING WOOD,
PONTITO, ITALY, 1987.
PHOTOGRAPH.

ALTHOUGH BORN IN
PONTITO MANY OF THE
VILLAGERS MOVED TO
OTHER CITIES AND
COUNTRIES AFTER THE
WAR IN SEARCH OF WORK.
MANY RETURNED TO THEIR
CHILDHOOD/FAMILY HOMES
IN PONTITO DURING THEIR
RETIREMENT. THEY SEEMED
TO UNDERSTAND FRANCO'S
BODY OF WORK—OR
PERHAPS HAVE SOME COM-
PLICITY WITH HIS DESIRE
TO HAVE THE VILLAGE AND
WAY OF LIFE CONTINUE
ON INTO THE FUTURE.

[2-5A] *opposite above left*

FRANCO MAGNANI,
LITTLE SQUARE, c.1980.
OIL ON CANVAS BOARD.

[2-5B] *opposite above right*

SUSAN SCHWARTZENBERG,
LITTLE SQUARE, 1988.
COMPOSITE PHOTOGRAPH.

A CENTRAL CROSSROAD
IN PONTITO, THIS SMALL
SQUARE WAS/IS AN
INFORMAL MEETING PLACE
WHERE VILLAGERS OFTEN
MEET AND SPEND TIME
TOGETHER. THE SMALL
IMPROMPTU BENCH IN THE
PHOTOGRAPH PROVIDED
A CLUE AS TO WHY
MAGNANI MADE THE
CENTRAL SECTION OF THE
SQUARE SO PRONOUNCED
IN HIS PAINTING.

THIS ACCENTUATION, OR
REGULARIZATION, IS A
TYPICAL VISUAL STRATEGY
TO BRING ATTENTION TO
THE PLACE—A POSSIBLE
REFERENCE TO ITS IMPORT-
ANCE IN THE VILLAGE. TO
MAKE SOMETHING MORE
REGULAR OR SYMMETRICAL
THAN IN REALITY IS
CONSIDERED A TYPICAL
MEMORY DISTORTION.

[2-6A] *opposite below left*

FRANCO MAGNANI,
MAGNANI HOUSE FRONT
STEPS, c.1986.
OIL ON CANVAS BOARD.

[2-6B] *opposite below right*

SUSAN SCHWARTZENBERG,
MAGNANI HOUSE FRONT
STEPS, 1987.
PHOTOGRAPH.

OFTEN WHEN REMEMBER-
ING THE PAST OBJECTS,
SPACES, AND RELATION-
SHIPS SEEM LARGER THAN
THEY ARE WHEN ENCOUN-
TERED IN THE PRESENT.
WHILE THIS IS A COMMON
MEMORY DISTORTION, IT
IS TELLING THAT IN THIS
IMAGE FRANCO PAINTS
HIMSELF AS A CHILD WITH
HIS MOTHER INSIDE THE
HOUSE. HE SAID HE WAS
PAINTING THE VILLAGE AS
HE RECALLED IT BEFORE
THE WAR, WHEN HE
WOULD HAVE BEEN SIX
OR SEVEN YEARS OLD.
FROM THE PERSPECTIVE OF
CHILDHOOD PONTITO'S
STONE BUILDINGS AND
STEPS WOULD HAVE HAD
APPEARED MONUMENTAL.

the scenes as remembered, the paintings displayed noticeable distortions: for example, the enlarged campanile and the way in which the picture plane had been "folded" to include parts of the village not easily witnessed from this hillside perspective [2–5A, 2–5B]. Certain comparisons displayed Franco's remarkable accuracy in both remembering and depicting: for example, the configuration of the roofs, the shadows, and the number of windows and other building details.

Although he had no formal training Franco used various pictorial conventions such as lightening or widening a walkway to move the eye through the composition. I later learned that this device could also be construed as a strategy for memory: moving through the village was part of the experience of remembering. To enhance or exaggerate the walkway in this way is often termed by psychologists and cognitive scientists as a sharpening strategy—a means by which our brains and mind select and enhance specific things to hold them in our memory.[4]

[2–7A]

FRANCO MAGNANI, STAIRS, c.1987. GRAPHITE ON BOARD.

[2–7B] *oposite*

SUSAN SCHWARTZENBERG, STAIRS, 1988. COMPOSITE PHOTOGRAPH.

A COMPOSITE RECON- STRUCTION OF THE SCENE APPROXIMATES THIS IMAGINATIVE VIEW CAPTURED IN MAGNANI'S DRAWING. TO RECONSTRUCT THIS VIEW I HAD TO PAN THE SCENE, TAKING SEVERAL PHOTOGRAPHS AS NO SINGLE PHOTOGRAPH COULD CAPTURE EVERY- THING IN THE DRAWING. MOST COGNITIVE SCIENTISTS AGREE THAT MEMORY IS A RECONSTRUCTIVE PROCESS WHERE THE PAST IS OFTEN BUILT FROM MANY EXPERI- ENCES AND PAST RECOLLECTIONS.

While Franco included few people in his images, their inclusion was instructive. In one painting the young Franco plays on the stairs within the protective view of his mother who is visible within the house in the background [2–6A, 2–6B]. That it depicts Franco in his youth may suggest why he rendered the village as larger than it really was. His sense of scale also reflects his age at the purported time of the picture. In responding to a question about this aspect of the image he made it clear that he knew things in the village had changed even as he was growing up—but that for telling his visual story he had consciously chosen this time before the war, when his life and family were intact.

This view from Franco's childhood room puzzled me at first, because there was no position in the room from which to match the view shown in the painting [see 2–1A, 2–1B]. Certain station points produced approximately similar views, but only by leaning out of the window and moving around in the room could I put the entire scene together and see the

church and roof of the neighboring house. In time I realized that many of the images were composites: in this case compilations of experiences accrued in that room over time. Cognitive scientists refer to memory as a "reconstructive process."[5] The perceptual psychologist Rudolf Arnheim has stated that: "A perceptual act is never isolated; it is only the most recent phase of a stream of innumerable similar acts, performed in the past and surviving in memory."[6] Thus, memory is always an imaginative reconstruction of the past, playing a strong role in building one's story or identity, a process termed "autobiographical memory."[7]

Other places shown in Franco's paintings were impossible to capture in a single photograph as well. In this narrow passage, with my back to the wall, I took a series of photographs from which I later created a montage [2–7A, 2–7B]. This visualization suggested another instance of the recollection process, one which expressed or described the workings of our visual system. The lenses of our eyes are very imperfect, with true focus only within a very narrow cone of vision. In addition, the image received in the eye is inverted and reversed. In order to see we must scan a scene to capture its many facets, and from this the brain surmises the visual totality before us. In fact, we see very little: instead, we rely on memory to complete the picture and re-present an image we can recognize.

The project team also met with Italian social psychologist Phillip Zimbardo. While viewing these comparison images he looked back and forth several times before pointing to the little impromptu bench visible in the photograph; it was missing from the painting. He said that the bench was a clue to how the small square or crossroad might presently be used by the villagers as a place to meet. The painting also suggested this visually in the manner in which the square was decisively depicted [see 2–5A, 2–5B]. He noted that in Italy the piazza is the central point in every village or city, the place where people often meet and collect informally. Franco's handling of the space heightened our attention to this square, its deliberate regularity suggesting that something important happens here. Multiple views of the square showed the center of village life through which people passed every day. They frequently sat and chatted on the bench or brick walls—and while I was photographing, they offered both their comments and services as my assistants. Embodied then in these images were not only the distortions of universal memory and the sharpening strategies used as compensation, but also the particular story of the village's history and culture of daily use.

As I worked I met more villagers and learned more about how they lived, and how many of them had returned to this village of their childhoods. Although they now lived a more rural life than they might experience in an urban center, here they were at home. There seemed to be some complicity between Franco's love of the place and those of the current villagers, and I suspected that Franco's recollections were unknowingly shared by others. In that sense the painting project represented a collective and perhaps unconscious understanding of a way of life, a memorial to a place and way of life now gone.

This image embodies an essential purpose of human memory [2–8]. Some comparisons were very difficult to bring into accord and no sequence of photographs clearly represented the view. For example, in this rather telescoped scene the little building on the right was today mostly a hole in the ground filled with some brick and rubble; however, the villagers assured me this was the same spot shown in the painting. It was once a small chapel that had been used as a medical aid station during the war. Further in the distance stood another chapel, today hardly visible through a pile of logs, and even further in the distance lay the mountains. I dutifully made several pictures recording the mountains and chapels although they had nothing of the feeling and relationships depicted in Franco's painting. When I showed my comparisons to Franco he said, "Yeah, I know. What can I say? I used to go the mountains with my father and I loved that very much." This image wasn't about exactness, but instead about emotionally ordered detail depicting a way of life, an existential context—something the cognitive scientists call "qualia," what in the study of consciousness they call the "hard question."[8] We may now be able to understand how memory is processed and recalled. But we have only less certain knowledge about why something possesses a special feeling or quality—aspects less easily explained by descriptions of the electrochemical system scientists use to define the mind.

BRAIN

Ten years after the exhibition of Franco Magnani's paintings and photographs the Exploratorium opened a larger exhibition of artworks, exhibits, and programs exploring the cognitive, biological, personal, and collective/social aspects of memory. Included in the exhibition were dissections of sheep brains—performed daily—that allowed visitors to see the structure of a brain very similar to that of the human. Another exhibit recorded electrochemical activity in the nerve cell of a sea slug to present the language by which nerve cells communicate.[9]

The brain is truly a black box. Unlike many of the body's organs it doesn't resemble what it does. The eye has a lens that focuses light on a layer of receptor cells, the heart and stomach resemble pumps, and the lungs are lightweight and move air somewhat like a bellows. But brains don't look like

[2–8]

FRANCO MAGNANI, *TO THE MOUNTAINS*, 1987 OIL ON CANVAS BOARD.

NO SETS OF PHOTOGRAPHS WERE ABLE TO REPRESENT THIS PAINTING. THE DISTANCE TO THE MOUNTAIN WAS TOO FAR, THE TWO CHAPELS HAD BEEN ALTERED OVER TIME, AND NO PATHWAY WAS AS CLEARLY DEFINED AS IN THE PAINTING. THIS ROUTE TO THE MOUNTAINS—WHICH FRANCO LATER DESCRIBED AS ONE HE WOULD TAKE WITH HIS FATHER TO GATHER MUSHROOMS AND FIREWOOD—IS CLEARLY DEPICTED IN THIS IDYLLIC VIEW.

thinking. The convolutions are described as being "efficient" but how perceptions, imagination, decisions, feelings, and emotions are processed is not readily apparent. Historically philosophers, psychologists, and neuroscientists have used various metaphors to describe how the brain goes about processing, storing, and retrieving past memories. The most common of these are spatial metaphors which may be assigned to two primary groups: as a container, or as a process within the container.

Aristotle first described the brain and memory as working like a soft wax tablet, where memory resides and fades. Others include metaphors of a more mechanical nature: a file cabinet, a magic tablet, cameras, gramophones, the rooms in a house, caves, theaters, and computers. Plato suggested a more whimsical, or some say more natural, view where thoughts, like birds, fly in and out—some remain in store while others only flit through our consciousness. Forests and streams, landscapes, oceans, and weather patterns are other natural phenomena used as metaphors for the brain. Current thinking in the cognitive- and neurosciences proposes that memory is

a reconstructive process and that no perception exists in any particular place—as it would in a file cabinet—but rather that impressions are constantly re-stimulated and re-combined. Every thought and recollection is constantly conjured and reconsidered. In more controversial metaphors memory or consciousness is considered as an emergent property of a dynamic system of nerve cell activity—like a weather pattern—where reality is a honed field of impressions and assumptions.[10]

PERSONAL WORK

In my own work I have explored the relationship between memory and history in the public realm, considering how inserting an idea into a landscape can generate a conversation or influence a point of view. In 1996 I published a pocket-sized tour guide to San Francisco's Market Street. Rather than a guidebook that featured famous people, places, or specific moments in the city's history, the book took form primarily as a visual narrative related in photographs—mostly my own, but also drawn from various San Franciscan archives—then coupled with excerpts from conversations collected along Market Street [2–9]. Sometimes I talked with people about San Francisco, its history, and what it was like to live there; sometimes we discussed jobs, economics, home, family, or the world situation—in all, life and its uncertainties. At times my encounters involved professionals, others did not; some people with whom I talked were homeless, some were tourists. My simple thought was: if you listened to the voices of people on the street, what could you learn about a place? How did the assembled thoughts of people coalesce as the idea of a city? I found that everyone knew something about San Francisco, and that by combining these voices I could produce an idiosyncratic impression of the time and space of the city. In addition the project proposed a way to depict collective memory, or a

[2–9]
SUSAN SCHWARTZENBERG, *CENTO*, PAGE SPREAD FROM "THE ARCHIVE," 1996.
OFFSET LITHO, PUBLISHED BY THE SAN FRANCISCO ART COMMISSION.

CENTO IS A MULTIPLE-VOICED VISUAL AND LITERARY NARRATIVE, A CONVERSATION ABOUT SAN FRANCISCO'S MARKET STREET. "THE ARCHIVE" PRESENTS SUBJECTS WHO WERE INTERVIEWED AND ASKED TO DESCRIBE THEIR IDEA OF THE ARCHIVE. THEY INCLUDED THE PHOTO ARCHIVIST OF THE SAN FRANCISCO PUBLIC LIBRARY, A PRIVATE DETECTIVE, AN ARCHEO-LOGIST, AN ECOLOGIST AND AN HISTORIAN.

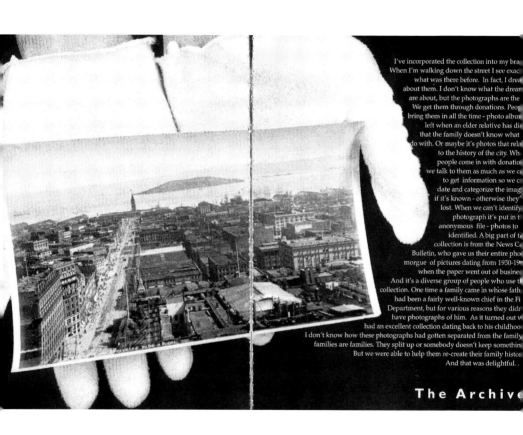

I've incorporated the collection into my bra
When I'm walking down the street I see exac
what was there before. In fact, I drea
about them. I don't know what the drea
are about, but the photographs are the
We get them through donations. Peop
bring them in all the time - photo albu
left when an elder relative has di
that the family doesn't know what
do with. Or maybe it's photos that rela
to the history of the city. Wh
people come in with donatio
we talk to them as much as we c
to get information so we c
date and categorize the imag
if it's known - otherwise they'
lost. When we can't identify
photograph it's put in t
anonymous file - photos to
identified. A big part of t
collection is from the News C
Bulletin, who gave us their entire pho
morgue of pictures dating from 1930-19
when the paper went out of busine
And it's a diverse group of people who use t
collection. One time a family came in whose fath
had been a fairly well-known chief in the Fi
Department, but for various reasons they didr
have photographs of him. As it turned out v
had an excellent collection dating back to his childhoo
I don't know how these photographs had gotten separated from the family
families are families. They split up or somebody doesn't keep somethin
But we were able to help them re-create their family histor
And that was delightful. .

The Archive

"psychic" sense of space.[11] The book, published in 1996, is called *cento* because a "cento" is a style of writing constructed by the contributions of many authors.

The Rosie the Riveter Memorial (2000), designed and produced in collaboration with the landscape architect Cheryl Barton, honored female workers of World War II. Though the memorial took a national perspective, it incorporated many voices and stories from those who had worked in the shipyards of the San Francisco Bay Area. The site lay on the shoreline of Richmond, California, where sixty years before an enormous Kaiser Industries complex had built Liberty and Victory ships. At the onset of the project we looked at numerous photographs and read accounts of the many workers who had been employed in the Richmond/Kaiser yards. The site today is a complex of condominiums, light industries, parks, and a pleasure boat harbor. In response to the changed conditions and uses our project wanted to evoke some sense of the scale of work once undertaken there. We based the sculptural elements of the memorial on the prefabricated components of the ships that were craned to massive shipways on the waterfront and assembled there. The memorial is a minimal construction supporting selected texts and images that in simple fragments narrate pieces of the site's history to those walking on a path which marks the length of one of the 700 ships built on the site during those turbulent times.

For years the City of Richmond had hoped to create this memorial and in preparation a Rosie Trust had already been created. A list of names of the women who had worked there would serve as the foundation of the commemoration. Women were invited to send their own names as well as the names of others, but instead, many described their work or sent snapshots to the archive. The women told of their new

[2-10A]
SUSAN SCHWARTZENBERG AND THE OFFICE OF CHERYL BARTON, ROSIE THE RIVETER MEMORIAL, RICHMOND, CALIFORNIA, 2000.
[SUSAN SCHWARTZENBERG]

[2-10B]
ROSIE THE RIVETER MEMORIAL.
[LEWIS WATTS]

THE PROJECT LINKED THE PREFABRICATION PROCESS OF BUILDING SHIPS TO THE RE-CONSTRUCTIVE PROCESS OF HUMAN MEMORY. MANY OF THE WOMEN EXPRESSED REGRET AT FORGETTING SO MUCH OF THEIR EXPERIENCES, BUT ONCE THEY BEGAN TALKING OR HEARING THE STORY OF OTHERS THEY BEGAN TO RECOL-LECT AND SHARE THEIR STORIES, CONTRIBUTING TO A SHARED NARRATIVE OF AN HISTORIC EVENT.

freedom, challenging tasks, the people with whom they had worked and socialized, 24-hour dance clubs, and the bands they listened and danced to first-hand, but they also often apologized for fear they had forgotten an important date or the last name of a fellow worker. Slowly over the next years we gathered these fragmented impressions and reassembled and embedded them into the sidewalk, image ladders, and sculptural pieces of the memorial [2–10A, 2–10B].

We associated the idea of the prefabricated ship parts with the reconstructive process of human memory. In numerous visits to the site since the project's completion I've watched people make their way along the walk, engaging with the fragments that seem to successfully provoke interest and possibly even generate a dialog between the past and present, as well as the dialog between the extended generations of child, parent, and grandparent that visit together. Perhaps the memorial is more of a construct in the mind than an actual object in the landscape. When visitors reach the shoreline they turn back and often appear to realize that the pieces of the memorial cohere as the form of a ship. Or perhaps they realize that they now know something of the history and personal experiences that took place here—a new consideration of the dynamic aspects of the social landscape.

In much of my work lies the idea that there is a psychology embedded in every place. The psychologist Ernest Becker wrote that:

> The body is one of the things in which our true feelings
> are located, but it is not the only one ... Least of all is
> the self limited to the body. A person literally projects or
> throws himself out of the body, and anywhere at all.[12]

In other words, our inner existence (mind) is incredibly entangled with the exterior world—in the things we make and in the phenomenological world in which we live.

NOTES

1 The initial exhibits at the Exploratorium concentrated on perception and physics—or the ways the physical world works. The perception exhibits explored the physiology of the eye and how it mechanically retrieves information and relays it to the brain for processing. The cognition exhibits take advantage of recent research in cognitive neuroscience, which suggests that the senses are really extensions of the brain, and how difficult it is to see or hear things we do not already know. These exhibits explore attention, emotion, and decision-making.

2 The Memory exhibition explored human memory through the artwork of Franco Magnani—what the extraordinary works of one individual (comparing the painted scenes with the photographs) might reveal about the remembering process. Another aspect of this exhibition of comparative works that was present, but not formally investigated, concerned observations about the nature of reality and experience as recorded via these different mediums.

3 As the project developed we initiated a correspondence with the neurologist Dr. Oliver Sacks and invited him to be the keynote speaker for the opening of the exhibition, after which he came back regularly to talk with Franco to learn more about his story and memory. He wrote an article in 1988 for *The New Yorker* that was developed further in a thought-provoking essay on Franco, memory, identity, and the human mind entitled "The Landscape of His Dreams." It was included in his book of essays *An Anthropologist on Mars*, *Seven Paradoxical Tales*, New York: Alfred Knopf, 1995, pp. 153–187.

4 Most contemporary psychology textbooks include discussions of memory distortions and forgetting with various strategies for memory improvement. In *Visual Thinking* Rudolph Arnheim discusses the ways by which various memory improvement strategies, including sharpening and leveling techniques, are linked to pictorial and compositional conventions within the visual arts. Rudolph Arnheim, *Visual Thinking*, Berkeley: University of California Press, 2nd edn 1972, pp. 81–83.

5 In a chapter on memory distortions the cognitive scientist Daniel Schacter discusses Freud's observations and questions about memory, and clinically how difficult it was to really know if someone had accurately remembered an event from the past. Daniel L. Schacter, *Searching for Memory: The Brain, The Mind, and The Past*, New York: HarperCollins, 1996, pp. 100–101. Schacter attributes a subsequent study by Frederick Bartlett "as solving this problem." Bartlett concludes that remembering is an imaginative reconstruction of past experiences, rather than an exact replica. Bartlett's study and findings were published in his 1932 monograph *Remembering*.

6 Arnheim, *Visual Thinking*, p. 80.

7 See Schacter, *Searching for Memory*.

8 John R. Searle, *The Mystery of Consciousness*, New York: New York Review of Books, 1997. Searle's book and controversial argument categorizes human subjectivity as a biological phenomenon, which he believes should be at the center of the study of consciousness. Although Searle is not the first person to use the term "qualia," this book is a compelling argument for it.

9 Memory opened in 1998 and began traveling to science centers throughout the U.S. in 1999. For a description of the exhibition and other online exhibits visit http://www.exploratorium.edu/memory/

10 See H. L. Roediger, "Memory Metaphors in Cognitive Psychology," in *Memory and Cognition*, Austin, TX: Psychonomic Society Publications, 1980; Douwe Draaisma, *Metaphors of Memory, A History of Ideas about the Mind*, Cambridge: Cambridge University Press, 2000; Robert Port and Tim van Gelder, eds, *Mind as Motion, Explorations in the Dynamics of Cognition*, Cambridge, Mass.: MIT Press, 1998.

11 The project was also a lament against urban redevelopment. The city was transforming around me—and it seemed urgent to preserve some collective sense of what it was. Now, ten years later, the street and its space have dramatically changed. Susan Schwartzenberg, *cento*, San Francisco: San Francisco Arts Commission, 1996.

12 Ernest Becker, *The Birth and Death of Meaning*, New York: The Free Press, 2nd edn, 1971, pp. 32–33.

In his recent book *Imagining Eden*, Lyle Gomes observes of his collection of panoramic landscape photographs that in a deep sense, all the images pursue that fundamental quest for a primal nature in which we belong—though they record a number of different places.[1] Selecting among these beautiful photographs, we may construct a continuum from the ascent of a sculpted angel out of the verdure, through photos of draped human figures standing guard in a tunneled wildness, to images of heroic figurative sculpture and attendant benches promenading through an arcade of shaped trees, shifting then to a carefully framed dormer marking out inhabitation within a low roof set among foliage. The progression may culminate in a round, room-sized keep—a surrogate human presence in the larger landscape. These may be seen as talismans of primary ways that people imagine their relation to place [3–1A, 3–1B].

"Place," as I understand it, refers to spaces that can be remembered, that we can imagine, hold in the mind, and consider. They are territories that can be lived in with special satisfaction because they resonant with associations that engage our interest. Places bring things to mind. As designers our task is to find ways to make places that are especially memorable and to consider how we may absorb and direct attention through the thoughtful making of places. As authors of the forms and relationships through which people move, and to which they attend, we need to ask what should be brought to mind and what range of observations are likely to be discovered there. The experience of place is infused with memory; echoes of previous visits, expectations, and recollections invoked by similar places, as well as images, and descriptions in advertisements and books, and on the internet. All of these have prepared us (or enticed us) to visit; all present themselves for comparison in our minds.

The memories lodged in places range from incidents of personal biography to highly refined and extensively interpreted segments of cultural lore, vested in the forms and the elements of ornament with which the place is made. These traces of patterns, which are based in understandings shared by participants in a culture, are given specific interpretation in a particular place. The experience of place within architecture, landscape, and cities is in some sense made of memories.

What role do those memories have in the conduct of our lives, and more particularly, in our professional lives?

How are memories embedded in buildings and landscapes by their designers—and by those who use and experience them?

What characteristics of place encourage the attachment of memories?

Imagine a building as a magnet for associations, then imagine those associations symbolized by Post-it notes or "stickies." Is the mind better served by layering them, thereby transforming the appearance of the building? Or is it better served by ordering and absorbing the notes into clusters and groups? In the past, buildings were often made with generic "files"—rooms in a memory palace, if you will—into which items of related import could be placed. To harvest ideas implanted in places by those who originally made them requires a kind of empathy; an act of recognition or interpretation, a playing out of the thoughts of the person(s) who placed them there. This requires at least a period of reflection if not scholarship.

Memory is at work not only in places built for recall, but in the ways that we encounter and experience buildings and spaces in everyday life. Place, I repeat, is space that can be remembered—that you can hold in the mind and consider. It is this capacity for being held in the mind that allows places to accrue significances that are both intimate and public. They dwell in the minds of individuals, yet through incorporating elements of common experience, they help in the development of shared conceptions that bind our thoughts together.

Spaces become memorable in two ways: through formal structures with special coherence or power, and through events that take place rooted in a location—events that happen with such intensity, or are so frequently repeated, that they lend vividness to what surrounds them and invoke our memories of that place. It is the duality of these sources that sometimes makes the designation of "historic" buildings or places puzzling. They are places that can play a part in reconstructing histories, histories of architecture and histories of more general importance to the culture. They may be preserved because they are exceptionally well conceived and crafted, or they may be cherished because something happened within them that the culture (or its guardians) wish us to remember in a context that carries with it the associations of contemporary events. Memories come in clusters, not units.

Good places are structured so that they attract and hold memories; they are sticky—or perhaps you would rather say magnetic. To make places that attract and hold in this way is both more difficult and easier than you might imagine. Efforts to make them have frequently been led astray. Some buildings seem so intent on controlling our reactions to programmatic purpose that they are rejected by our affections and wind up unassimilated; or sometimes buildings are so wrapped in gratuitous gestures that they fail to genuinely engage our attention.

The difficulty often lies in the conflict between professional doctrine regarding the ways things should be made, and the experience of places that people commonly enjoy. Seeking to make each place a singular, memorable work of art often makes the insistence of its vocabulary resistant to the attachment of memories—to the full engagement of the people who use and live with the building. This error was compounded by architectural schools with programs intended to strip students of any personal meanings they bring to their assigned task of designing with pure forms. Intended or not, this practice suggested to several generations of professionals that personal memories were worthless (their own and those of others) and that only the pure rationality of construction could lead them to design with clarity and panache. Fortunately, this view is now being replaced by a more complex under-standing of sources and motivations, along with a flowering of available technical means.

THE DOME AND THE FRAME

Considering ways that buildings can be made to hold and direct our attention leads quickly to examining two of the oldest architectural elements: the dome and the frame. Domes, the expansion to heroic size of the most fundamental act of surrounding the body, have been a mainstay of symbolic expression in both Western and Islamic architecture. Like pyramids their attraction as symbolic form is evident; they are centered on a single hierarchical point, and their form is "eternal"; that is to say, their appearance is fundamentally unaffected by the contingencies of viewing location, appearing constant from various views and approaches. They are forms which are easily identified and shared, yet require considerable investment to build.

The near opposite of the immutable form of the dome or pyramid is the four post aedicule—the person-centered "little house" formed by the uprights of a porch or colonnade. When surrounded by columns or piers that frame your view, each step you take changes the visual field, altering the per-ception of your surroundings. You become an active agent in establishing the experience of the place.

Frames of course can be used in many ways to identify and control particular views, or places of entry and outlook, but in the end they depend on your engagement and location: you must position yourself to use them effectively and you can always choose to play your own game. Buildings and groups of buildings that employ both the constancy of the dome and the variable experiences afforded by moving among columns and framed openings have a particularly strong chance of securing your attention at several scales while establishing a context that is both hierarchical and capable of offering and absorbing differing kinds of experience and memory.

The San Francisco Palace of Fine Arts (Bernard Maybeck, 1915)—a great domed pavilion set beside a reflecting lagoon—is an excellent example of the dynamics between constant geometries and the shifting vantage points created by spaced elements through which you may move [3–2]. The dome barely changes aspect as you shift position, but the frame through which you see it changes radically as you move. The great marching columns along its sides encompass and modulate your view as you pass among them. This is amplified by the ways in which the plans of the passage and the building behind it employ a radius that is centered differently from that of the dome; as a result the architrave above you creates constantly differing angles against the sky. The dynamics are further elaborated by the syncopation of piers and grouped elements that have a rhythm far richer than simple repetition. On site you can weave in and out among the columns and piers, around and under the dome, and along the edge of the lagoon. Even if viewed from across the water on the opposite side of the lagoon, the background colonnade keeps shifting

in its relation to the domed center, creating an aspect that refreshes perception.

The domed building itself remains constant only at its top and around its drum, where mythological scenes are on constant view (albeit inscrutable to the mostly untrained eyes of today.) Great arches open to the interior and through to the back. The highly contrasted and alternating play of darks and lights, of solids and openings, invites the eye to enter and to see the world (again) through colossal arched frames that appear to shift slowly as the body moves.

All this contributes to the compelling attraction of the Palace of Fine Arts. It has a constant presence and elements that affirm your agency and challenge your thought as your vantage points or attention shifts. The detail and ornament of the structures carry traces of both ancient orders and systems of craft and the inventiveness of their creator's mind: torsos of women face mysteriously away from view and look downward into planters set within the clusters of piers, while Corinthian column capitals executed in vigorous molding also carry subliminal suggestions of ancient bird-like heads [3–3].

The landscape near the building furthers this diversity and capacity for creating memorable experience and associations. Its pockets of vegetation have multiple origins and are cared for with varied intent. The immediate edges close to the base are romantically wild and full of branches. A row of redwoods against the back wall tries (in vain) to be columnar like the great cast Corinthians in the colonnade before them. The pool has been tidied and bordered on the opposite side in a way that contrasts to the wild edge near the building. The lagoon hosts at least three major species of bird (feathered in

[3–2]

BERNARD MAYBECK, PALACE OF FINE ARTS, SAN FRANCISCO, CALIFORNIA, 1915. VIEW ACROSS THE LAGOON. [DONLYN LYNDON]

[3–3]

PALACE OF FINE ARTS, SAN FRANCISCO, CALIFORNIA. [DONLYN LYNDON]

deep black, white, and mottled gray), all very active emblems of a larger natural order. The lawn beyond hosts picnics, lounging, and "I've been there!" photographs centered on the dome. The long blank arcing wall that is background to the dome borders an exhibition space, strangely inaccessible to view, which for now holds the incredibly vibrant life of the San Francisco Exploratorium—a challenge to any melancholy that the architecture might evoke. Beyond this, of course, is the memory available in pictures and books telling us that this great space was a momentous part of the great 1915 Panama-Pacific International Exposition that celebrated the opening of the Panama Canal.[2]

The mind holds the dome and the lagoon. The rest re-animates the experience each time and allows for the reinvention of your relationship to its wonders. The whole is as close as it gets to the Charles Moore fantasy drawing that he and I used as the frontispiece for our book *Chambers for a Memory Palace*—a complex fusion of remembered classical form, encompassing nature and invitations to inhabit [3–4].[3]

The San Francisco City Hall, on the other hand, topped by a dome of academic correctitude, stands conventionally

[3–4] *below*
CHARLES MOORE,
THE TOWER OF BECQUIA, 1984.
WATERCOLOR.
[COURTESY OF CHARLES MOORE FOUNDATION]

[3–5] *opposite*
FRANK GEHRY,
GUGGENHEIM MUSEUM,
BILBAO, SPAIN, 1997.
[DONLYN LYNDON]

THE TOWER OF BECQUIA

as a rather grand symbol of city government. It also carries an important note of caution regarding the ways in which the significance of such symbols can be altered by experience, or even by the stories that derive from and build on experience. The interior of the City Hall is a great rotunda of public gathering dominated by a sculptural marble stairway that ascends grandly towards the ceremonial rooms of govern- ment on the second floor. The splendor of that gesture, however, is altered by the recollection—still present in many people's minds, if only from news photos—of the McCarthy era when demonstrators assembled there were literally washed down the stairs with fire hoses. This alternate story lends an indelible cast to the experience of the place.

There is a polarity between symbols like these, qualified by experience, and experience held in place by forms that become iconic symbols. Frank Gehry's Disney Hall in Los Angeles strikes me as the latter. All that shimmering titanium surface and dazzling light is finally held in place by the focus of the stage and performance inside—for those able to attend.

On the other hand, there is not much clarifying anchor inside the Guggenheim Museum at Bilbao, an earlier Gehry

work, whose celebrated form is held in place by its position between the city and the river. The latter has large elements of infrastructure that comport with the scale of Gehry's forms, alongside fanciful visions of passing ships. It is all complemented by artfully formed walks around the perimeter and through the adjoining park, and is constantly revivified by the shifting qualities of light on the building's glittering surfaces. Both the museum object and the place that it animates are subjects of attraction and magnets for memory [3–5].

Here again is a continuing dialog between centering—as in the stable form of the dome or pyramid, or in Bilbao's vibrant dynamism of a singular unexpected form—and the drastic changes in visual field and information wrought by moving around and within the encompassing context.

SETTING MEASURE TO PLACE

The Maison Carrée in Nîmes, France, built during the reign of the Romans, is one of the best preserved classical Roman structures. It has a simple plan, almost an ideogram, whose closed box of a cella—which houses the god—plays against an open, spacious porch with four Corinthian columns on a side. Pediments at each end terminate a simple gable roof. The whole is raised on a podium about two meters above the ground, reached by broad stairs that ascend beneath the pediment. The building is separated from adjoining buildings and streets by a recessed paved area—now a public plaza but originally a closed compound. The walls of the building, like the porch, are measured along their sides by an insistently repetitive spacing of columns and applied half columns.

The Corinthian order of the columns claims this provincial building as an outpost of Roman administration and classical culture. The totality of the image, grand in scale and correctly adorned with stone carving, speaks to the most primal image of a structure inhabited by authority. It was probably this quality that attracted Thomas Jefferson so intensely that he sought to reincorporate its form in the State House of Virginia some 1700 years later.

The 1993 Carré d'Art, a museum and library designed by Norman Foster, borrows from the cultural authority of Maison Carrée, its neighbor [3–6]. It too is dominated by measure, a regular spacing of thin concrete columns that create bays of comparable certainty. Whereas rich classical carving articulated the cornice-to-sky relation of the earlier building, the roof of the museum's porch is characterized by the striped light of a louvered sunshade. The columns, whose interval echoes the measure of the Maison Carrée, are thinner by far and less satisfying to stand by. These are not the forms of lusty Roman presence; the presentation here is one of precision and transparency, emblems of a technocratic order.

Today, the two buildings address each other across an urban space and their measured order gives memorable significance to the ordinary events of the city, plaza, and passing boulevard traffic. Together they construct an identifiably stately place in the city, one rooted not only in antiquity, but also in a vision of technological elegance and cultural aspiration. That place, nonetheless, gathers its energy from the vigorous form and deep history of the earlier, iconic temple.

How buildings establish their relation to surrounding buildings and landscape is a key determinant of the memories and insight that they yield. Buildings can merge with their surroundings or give shape to them. They can mark special locations within a complex or become an encompassing

frame for a spatial figure that itself becomes the centering, memory-gathering device.

The Place des Vosges in Paris illustrates the latter [3–7]. The nearly identical building facades and paced arcades were set out to frame a great square space in the early seventeenth century. They perform that task still, while the space itself has been further subdivided by subsequent generations with a circumambulating street, park fence, rows of clipped trees, formal plantings, and plots of grass and gravel paths, fountains and basins, and sandlots for play. All these features are given a center by a copse of tall linden trees that surround an equestrian sculpture of Louis XIII whose significance now recedes beneath accumulating memories of picnics, family outings, chance encounters, dalliances, and lonely observation. The strict form of Place des Vosges gives it pride of place in a richly varied urban setting; the conventional but well-calibrated divisions within that frame create opportunities for individuals to choose their own forms of engagement with the place and the clustering of private memories.

The central organizing figure that provided the strategy for the New Pembroke dormitories at Brown University is less absolute, more riven with adjustments to the circumstances and context of the site. We (MLTW/Lyndon Associates) arranged the complex in room clusters of varying sizes, each accessed by its own entry and stair. The two most important determinants in the massing of the buildings were an abstract cross-axial figure internal to the complex and the varied character of the two differing streets that the complex adjoins.

Each of the street faces of the building has a form that evokes memories to support its place in the city. The walls

[3–6]
MAISON CARRÉE,
ROMAN, c.16 BCE;
NORMAN FOSTER,
CARRÉ D'ART,
NÎMES, FRANCE, 1993.
[DONLYN LYNDON]

[3–7]
PLACE DES VOSGES,
PARIS, FRANCE, 1612+.
[DONLYN LYNDON]

edging the shopping street that adjoins the campus (Thayer Street) form a long and continuous frontage, organized with shops on the ground floor to connect with and reinforce the life of the town beyond. To recall the traditional urban structure—with its characteristic dark-green metal shop fronts at the base of red-brick buildings—there is a two-storey band of green glazed bricks that marks out the semblance of a commercial facade within the larger mass of housing. Along residential Bowen Street, on the other hand, smaller buildings and garden walls are closer in scale to the large houses they face at the edge of the campus.

The New Pembroke buildings surround two courts, one with a passage under the building to Thayer Street (since closed by an unsympathetic or unknowing administration). Three of the cardinal faces of the other, more distinct court are formed by building elements surfaced in red glazed brick. A large sculpted portal forming the fourth side marks the transition between the two spaces [3–8]. Terraces reach out and connect to these courts, bringing people out in good weather into a common surround. Each entry to the complex connects to this space and all the levels of the building have at least

one terrace where people are likely to appear, as though on an elevated stage or in the boxes of a theater [3-9].

Each of these terraces is a threshold to the commonality of the court, offering places to linger, gather, and converse—to generate memories. Being at the convergence of most paths through the complex, the gate supports the formation of a community of rooms and creates ample opportunities for chance encounter among residents. *Skygate*, by Alice Wingwall, is an openwork steel frame inhabited by sun-capturing configurations of painted steel tubing that laces the court with shifting shadows cast by its frame. It is a mark in the campus landscape awaiting individual interpretation and associations with the events of the court. It is a threshold for the imagination.[4]

The device that forges these disparate elements into a coherent memorable identity is the imposition of a strict axial geometry that controls the plan. It is a geometry that becomes absorbed into the positioning of various elements, (portal, entry bays, stairs, and tiered terraces) until the spatial figure itself disappears. But the underlying relationships are secured, even as each part addresses its own conditions.

[3-8] *opposite*
ALICE WINGWALL AND MLTW/LYNDON ASSOCIATES, *SKYGATE*, NEW PEMBROKE DORMITORIES, BROWN UNIVERSITY, PROVIDENCE, RHODE ISLAND, 1974.
[CERVIN ROBINSON]

[3-9] *right*
MLTW/LYNDON ASSOCIATES, NEW PEMBROKE DORMITORIES, BROWN UNIVERSITY, PROVIDENCE, RHODE ISLAND.
[DONLYN LYNDON]

Places of greater extent, places that are not the works of individual architects or landscape architects, invoke a different set of questions about memory. Elements of the public realm usually carry many initiatives, palimpsests of the imaginations that have been brought to the site and invested there. These, of course, become contentious over time, as new insights and interests compete in the larger arena. The public places easily held in the mind express wholeness, places like the Place des Vosges. But our cities have become harbors of a much more complex and fragmented culture now, places that engage the attention of many in various roles. What does it take to harvest some semblance of common association in a society of this sort? Is it not through buildings and defined spaces that engage experience and absorb the actions of many, yet yield an object of remembrance?

What's needed is a reference—"ah yes I've been there" —but for what purposes? Is it for the stimulation of private interests and recollections, and the development of the individual? Or is it for the promotion of discourse through the sharing of images with mutual resonance? To be more than a stimulus for shopping, there must be explication, or at least presentation, of various aspects of our culture. Our situation in the natural and constructed worlds needs to be frequently brought to mind—as well as connections with our past; its glories as well as its missteps. We need remembrances of achievements that may sharpen and inform our own.

"It cannot teach us—history never can. But we can learn from it."[5] So Joseph Ryckwert states in his conclusion to *The Dancing Column: Order in Architecture*, a study of Greek architecture and the mimesis of the human body. This stands as a valuable referent for how we should proceed. Two works by Giancarlo De Carlo illustrate that process of learning— drawing on personal memory and investigation, as well as reaching into the common ground of shared experiences.

For many of us who have studied such places, the Campo and its tower in Siena have left an important mark in our minds. It is a place of very many qualities from which to learn: about enclosure and vigorous marking, about consistency in materials, sizes, and openings, about ritualistic performances, and the course of the sun across a bowl of space formed from the original topography, then dammed by a great civic building whose tower rises improbably high and blossoms into a marble lookout out at the top that commands the region.

Some years ago Giancarlo De Carlo entered a competition for creating a third tower for Siena (the Cathedral on the ridge has the second great, competing tower) marking a section of the city that for many serves as entry point. The slenderness of the tower he proposed is familiar to all who know the city; its development as form is not. His explorations for the Siena Tower explored new territory, seeking a structure that would be unexpectedly transparent, but in ways that would elaborate the experience of movement and outlook throughout the tower. These characteristics substitute for the numb rigidity of gravity seeking the ground. The structure owes much to the revolutionary spirit of Tatlin's constructivist vision of a *Monument to the Third International*, a project whose daring deeply moved De Carlo throughout his career.

The resulting form, while not built, remained a work of which De Carlo was very proud. It had its most direct descendent in the last project that he did realize—the so-called Blue Moon at the Lido in Venice. There are a number of ways in which architecture can afford greater participation by its inhabitants in their experience and forming of place. Among these possibilities is the use of elements which inhabitants can connect to their own lives. Such places may offer a wide array of choices rather than being subjected to a singular pattern of use and sequence of spaces determined by the architect. The architecture may also be made in a way that encourages and supports a variety of associations and interpretations.

De Carlo's Lido project illustrates the ways in which one project may provide a proliferation of paths and experiences and support for layers of meaning and memory [3–10]. The shoreline site occupies a crucial juncture in the structure of the community, the intersection of its two principal avenues. The commission requested the design for a Piazzale Buccintori, a place of public gathering, on the beach side of this intersec-tion. To De Carlo's great satisfaction the project has earned the local nickname "The Blue Moon," referring to a memorable nightclub and place of resort located on the site in the decades before World War II, which was pointlessly bombed by the Germans as they departed Venice at the end of the Occupation.

At its core the project constitutes a network of differing paths, each affording choices of outlook, shade, enclosure, degrees of effort in movement, and prospects for encounter with others using the locale. By choosing among and combin-ing these paths, inhabitants construct a variety of differing experiences such as bathing, sunning, eating, and viewing. These differing itineraries may seem inconsequential; yet the sequences they establish fill the vessels of the mind with daily content. The diversity, complexity, and episodic quality of the experiences that they afford are like the intricate, unfolding paths that lace through Venice itself—sewing the fabric of the city into a place of perpetual discovery.

[3–10]
GIANCARLO DE CARLO, PIAZZALE BUCCINTORI (THE BLUE MOON), VENICE, ITALY, 2004. PLAN.
[COURTESY STUDIO DE CARLO]

[3–11]
PIAZZALE BUCCINTORI (THE BLUE MOON), VENICE, ITALY.
[DONLYN LYNDON]

Those who move through and join in the pleasures of this place will bring differing expectations and associations. Their responses, though individualized, will yet be prompted by the character of the scenes that unfold, the people and things they encounter, and the nature of the forms that engage their attention (recollective in some parts of a ship deck, in some parts of exotic domes, in some parts of undulating sand and amphitheaters). An architecture that is richly participatory, however, goes beyond proffering a range of immediate physical experiences. It offers as well the prospects of reflection and association. It affords opportunities to make connections to a larger order in the community, to the history and ecology of the territory, and to the imaginations of the immediate community.

The structure that marks all this in the larger landscape is an unusual dome—constructed of steel framing and partially skinned with a wood lattice that is irregularly and somewhat inexplicably placed. A central mast supports a network of steel members that directly ties to De Carlo's Siena Tower design. The form of the dome will carry conventional landmark qualities, but the stability of perception it affords—appearing the same from all angles—is replaced here by ephemeral qualities. The great spire, piercing into the sky, echoes both Tatlin's tower and the masts of the once mighty Venetian fleet [3–11].

From this work we can learn to search for ways of thinking that can bring new things to our attention, while at the same time affording reflection on what we remember, what others recall and cherish, and what we ourselves store in the repositories of the built world. Most urgently we need to search for what can be made available, drawing strands of meaning through the structures within which we and others live our lives.

Clearly one of the ways that we come to new understandings is by shedding memories that have become confining, that have encircled and inhibited our capacity to act, change, and grow. The presence of memories in a place should not serve as armor encasing the living self but as a memory board into which new ideas and connections can he inscribed: storing them, presenting and representing them in the flow of everyday life. In our exchanges with a world that is far more complex than we can grasp, we need places where we can lodge hooks that can be used to secure common ground.

The metropolitan landscapes that are emerging all around us are even more complex. Certainly we can think of New York, or Chicago, or Tokyo as places, but we also know in that very instant that these are multiple places, that there are spaces there which we shall never know, yet which live with more or less certainty in the minds of their inhabitants. We also know that these myriads of places are bound into recognizable entities with some images that characterize the whole and become ways of thinking about their future. Examples are the sparkling media and great cultural resources of New York City that sweep from our mind the poverty and degradation in its metropolitan spread, or the wastelands of abandoned industrial cities where shrinkage is now being reclaimed as opportunities for recreation, reforesting, and the recovery of larger-scale ecological connections. All these can be revealed as sources of both change and continuity, memories, and prospects.

What places can and should bring to mind are the fecundity of nature, the importance of caring attention (both

personal and communal), the diverse imaginative reach of a
multitude of minds, the joys of human movement and activity,
and the reflective value of being at rest and profoundly located.
These, when brought to our attention and made a part of
our lives, can subvert (we must hope) even the maniacally
destructive impulses of ideologues—whatever their banners.

As Thomas Sieverts has written regarding the means
for understanding and working in the metropolitan landscape:

> It is not a matter of style (there are many different
> aesthetics), but of emotional ties to the environment
> as the prerequisite of deeper interest, responsibility, and
> care. It is this deep, fundamental connection to care
> and responsibility, which makes aesthetics so important.[6]

Emotional ties of this sort take place through the sorting
and realigning of memories, brought to mind by the forms and
inhabited spaces of the Edens we imagine and the built,
inhabited landscapes that become our earthly measure.

NOTES

1 Lyle Gomes, *Imagining Eden*, Charlottesville: University of Virginia Press, 2005.

2 The Exposition originally colonized this area of the city but all its other buildings have since been supplanted by what is now called the Marina District, its buildings full of simulated memories of Mediterranean villas.

3 Donlyn Lyndon and Charles Moore, *Chambers for a Memory Palace*, Cambridge, Mass.: MIT Press, 1994.

4 That the interpretation of this gate depends on the beholder has been well illustrated. When the *Architectural Review* published the project they referred to the pipes of the sculpture as stamens of a flower. This infuriated Alice Wingwall, who retorted that they had more to do with Athena Nike and rockets. (Personally, I found them recollective of the buxom nymphs adorning the gates of the Buddhist Stupa at Sanchi, India). In his review of the complex Robert Campbell won the prize, however. He referred to the courtyard as Neapolitan and the gate as a giant laundry

rack in its center. He got it exactly right: *Skygate* is waiting there for the dorm's inhabitants to hang out their memories.

5 Joseph Ryckwert, *The Dancing Column: Order in Architecture*, Cambridge, Mass.: MIT Press, 1996, p. 391.

6 Thomas Sieverts, "Metropolitan Landscapes: Attitudes, Research and Practice," *Places*, Vol.19:1 2007, p. 18.

[4]
Indelible Marker, Palimpsest, Thin Air

Alice Aycock

One of my favorite stories is "The Aleph" by Jorge Luis Borges. It is a story about obsessive memory, and in the story Borges muses about his life and ambition as an artist, writer, and poet. As a young man he falls in love with a very beautiful women by the name of Beatrice (she is called Beatriz in the Borges story) but she has no interest in him. He loves her desperately for years. In time she dies tragically and he is heartbroken by the realization that he has never been able to gain her love. So every year on the anniversary of her death he meets for dinner with Beatrice's cousin, trying to find out more about what she was like when she was young—just any tidbit of information he might learn about her. But each time Borges meets with the cousin—I believe his name was Daneri —her cousin only wants to talk about poetry and literature. This pattern continues for a number of years. And although Borges really finds this man quite boring, he puts up with it for the sake of the memory of Beatrice.

Finally, one night Daneri says to Borges: "I have a secret; it's in my basement. I want to share it with you. Go down there and lie in the dark at the bottom of the stairs—you will see a marvelous thing." Borges reluctantly agrees. He lies there in the dark, he hears the rats scurrying about, and he thinks this is a really stupid idea. But suddenly, after he has been in the basement for an hour or two, he sees what he describes as a "tear in the universe." It's about a half-centimeter in diameter. In this tear he sees everything that ever was, every-thing that is, and everything that will be. He goes on for pages describing what he sees. But at the end of this vision—which was sort of like a hologram—he jumps up and runs up the stairs. Daneri, who is standing there excitedly, asks: "What did you see? What did you think?" Borges doesn't know what to say; he is astounded; he is jealous; he is shocked; he just runs out of the house.

Some weeks later, Daneri calls and says: "The restaurant next door wants to expand and they are going to tear down my house—they're going to destroy this marvelous thing in the basement"—which he refers to as the Aleph. "Do something; go to the press. Please help me; do something about this."

Being the typical young artist who just cares about him-self, Borges does nothing and the house is destroyed—the Aleph, the secret in the basement, destroyed with it. Borges thinks he is done with the matter but about a year or two later, Daneri publishes an extraordinary poem in which he recreates the universe of the Aleph, recreates what he saw in the basement. And he becomes the successful new, rising-star writer.

Borges tells the story from a point in time many years later in which he reflects upon that event so long ago. He says the years have been wearing away the memory of what he saw in that basement, and finally, at last, the years have been wearing away the memory of Beatrice. I love this story for all kinds of reasons, and each time I tell it the story means something different to me. I think the years have begun to wear away the passion of my obsessive love affairs, but since I think of making love and making art as somewhat similar, each day I ask myself whether I can still call up that passion from deep down inside myself and that desire to try to recreate that tear in the universe.

And in many ways my early art was about memory— collective historical memory and individual experiential memory. A very early piece, *A Simple Network of Tunnels and Wells*, referred to underground spaces like basements and the emotions that are evoked by crawling around underground in the dark [4–1A, 4–1B]. For me it was about making an architectural sculpture which existed in the world, and at the same time creating something that relies on archaeology and the history of architecture, the romanticization of ruins, and photographs of ancient ruins, tombs, and tunnels in Greece, and Rome, and Egypt. It was an underground structure in which you would crawl in the dark, trying to remember once you got down there what you had seen above ground and the kind of structures you had encountered before the descent. The configuration appears at first to be simple and clear, geometric and rectilinear. But the actual experience is not. As you moved from light to dark you entered a much more mysterious place in which you must physically and psychologically engage the sculpture. And then you finally could emerge from below, joining thoughts and feelings about what is above with what is below.

When I was a young artist I made a series of drawings about imagining these physically and psychologically challenging

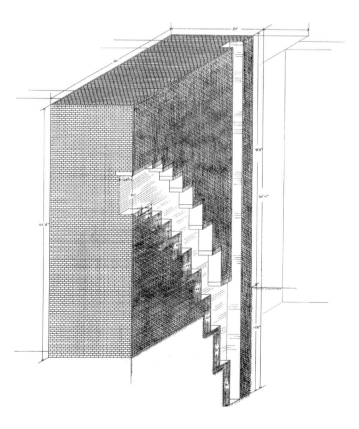

[4–1B]
ALICE AYCOCK,
*A SIMPLE NETWORK OF
UNDERGROUND WELLS
AND TUNNELS*
(DESTROYED),
MERRIEWOLD WEST,
FAR HILLS, NEW JERSEY,
1975.
[ALICE AYCOCK]

[4–2]
ALICE AYCOCK,
*MASONRY
ENCLOSURE:
PROJECT FOR A
DOORWAY,* 1976.
ISOMETRIC SECTION (B).
PENCIL ON VELLUM.
[JOHN FERRARI]

experiences. In a sense I was probably making monuments to my own fears about death; I was obsessed—and probably still am—about making a mark that would live past me.

And I imagined one of these works set in a desert somewhere—a vast, vast empty desert; perhaps the Egyptian desert [4–2]. And you would just come upon this structure like the materialization of a mirage. You would see it from a distance and there would be only a single door. And when you got there, you would build a ladder to get up to that door set high above in the brick masonry. Then you would begin to climb down inside, gauging your physical ability with each downward step—down, down, down, until you found yourself at the base of the pit. With each step you would have to ask yourself whether or not you could get back up again. There were many theoretical drawings, fantasies like a shantytown perhaps drawn from memories of vernacular wood buildings and ghost towns. In essence the landscape was always implied, as if it already existed and as if it would always be there. It was always going to be a place I could move into and domesticate.

Many of my early pieces were temporary works, such as *Five Walls* at Artpark, built on a pile of industrial spoils [4–3]. You entered a tunnel and climbed the walls using ladders, zigzagging into the air. Works from this period addressed notions of height and/or being beneath the ground, and the psychological and physiological experiences instigated by them. The projects were definitely sited, but unspecifically— although I also took for granted that there would always be enough land.

The *China Drawing* was also made in those early years as an artist. Its story concerns an old woman who wants to remember her life. She assigns doors to weeks, and then the doors become structures and the weeks become streets and the streets of doors become years. She thinks that by walking through this city that she built, she will be able to remember all the parts of her life, past and present. But only a few doors stand out over time, and the story is far from complete. The drawing was all about memory and forgetfulness. At one point in my life I had the absurd fantasy that one day I would really understand my life, like a narrative with a beginning, middle, and end. And there would be this kind of visual symbol at the end that would say: "This embodies your life!"—just like that.

At one point I returned to my mother's hometown in the coal regions of Pennsylvania. I looked at the houses in the town, typical American houses but also localized types. In *Project Entitled "I Have Tried to Imagine the Kind of City You and I Could Live in as King and Queen,"* the houses, based on these forms, were all connected by the old coal chutes—elements taken from the industrial landscape [4–4]. I gave them names from ancient Greek architecture. I never built the whole city, but I did get to build several of the structures at full scale. They were all temporary works and many of them were designed using the labyrinth or the maze as a structural model: you would go up and down towers, and you would dead end: and then you would go back the way you came. There was no clear path, no easy way to find a path [4–5].

In projects such as *The Large Scale Disintegration of Micro Electronic Memories* I thought about how I could envision and embody the structure of the mind with all its layered and labyrinthine connections—the mind as an electronic network. I couldn't really figure out how to do that, however. So I first made a series of drawings and then I built a work on the landfill that is now Battery Park City in New York. The structure of plywood and 2x4s was both labyrinthine and endless—it just went on and on and on, and it never really ended in completion. The structure ended only at the waterline and when time and money ran out. Some parts were completed and other parts were never finished; some parts even started to disintegrate during the short existence of the project. Works like this one were all very temporary—they were supposed to last only a couple of months—and they were made with very low budgets. I still think of the drawings for the Battery Park City work as something I want to return to in the vast chaos after the destruction of the World Trade Center. I am not really interested in what could be built on the site in the aftermath, but I am very interested in the chaotic way the buildings fell and the metaphorical implications of "worlds in collision" [4–6]. What fascinates me is the layering of structures and the physics of disorder or the order of chaos. Is it possible to inject that sense of chaos into a work which is planned and built from scratch?

By the mid-1980s, I had become increasingly aware that open land was not—as I first thought—in endless supply.

[4-3] *opposite*
**ALICE AYCOCK,
PROJECT ENTITLED
"THE BEGINNINGS
OF A COMPLEX ...
EXCERPT SHAFT #4 /
FIVE WALLS,"** 1977.
[ALICE AYCOCK]

[4-4] *below*
**ALICE AYCOCK,
PROJECT ENTITLED
"I HAVE TRIED TO
IMAGINE THE KIND
OF CITY YOU AND I
COULD LIVE IN AS
KING AND QUEEN,"**
1987.
ISOMETRIC VIEW.
INK ON PAPER.
[COURTESY LAUMEIER
SCULPTURE PARK]

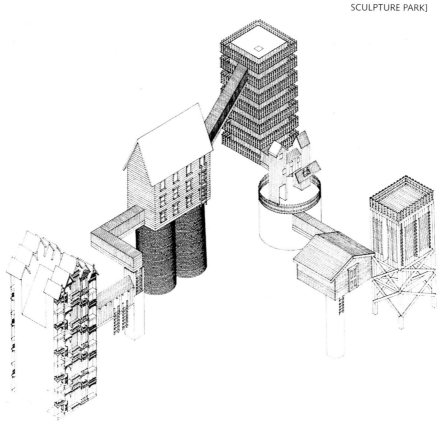

My fascination with invention and tool-making and the Industrial Revolution increased significantly in those years. I used to think of the aftermath of the Industrial Revolution primarily in academic terms, but now I realized there was much more to it than an abstract story: urban decay, machines, magic, science, Third World *favellas* and shantytowns, and the remnants of things we carelessly throw away. When making one piece in Japan I began to realize how over-urbanized the country was. Then I found this one little pristine lake where I sited my structure, where I tried to question the relation of thought to feeling. I found that in a sense the landscape existed more in the minds of people, in the memories of people, in the fantasies of people, and in the art of the past than in reality. To address my new concerns I felt that I had to leave these park-like pieces that had been built in an idealized, utopian situation; I needed to take on grittiness of the world.

In drawings I began to explore the idea of industrialization and its origins, and how civilization could begin with something like an arrowhead and end up with a hydrogen bomb. Was there any symbol or generic image that could contain or even communicate all of that? These new machine pieces had no function although they were about machines. But because they were machines I had to give them a function— like the task of catching or manufacturing ghosts. There was actually a French inventor who tried to make an electricity machine to make ghosts and bring back the dead. Early cinema and magic theater were all about creating apparitions. For me ghosts were actually a form of memories—things that you longed for and that you loved, and that you could no longer have for one reason or another—or perhaps that you had never had. The machines referred to alchemical and chemical apparatus and kitchen equipment, as well as a lot of references to electrical generation and electrostatic electricity (things stored in bottles) and early science experiments in general.

The Machine in the Garden was installed outside the library at Douglas College in New Jersey. The generally held image of central New Jersey is that of one vast urban wasteland with decaying rusty machines and highways and strip malls. In response, *The Machine in the Garden* drew on little bits and pieces of different types of experiments and scientific equipment. One of the works, *Collected Ghost Stories from the Workhouse,* resembled an oil refinery, with a lot of glass-within-glass and bottle-within-bottle elements [4–7]. While there was lot of fantasy in the projects, I also tried to use the architecture of industry—form and function—they seemed to be far more interesting than the everyday architecture then being built. To this day the refineries along the Jersey Turnpike bring me to my knees—despite all their pollution and decay.

I attended liberal art colleges as an undergraduate, as well as a graduate student in studio art, and I was required to write papers. One of these was a paper on the development of tumuli and mounded earth buildings as precedents for Bramante's circular, domed Tempietto in Rome. It was an unconscious cultural process of received memories and images that took place over thousands of years. As I worked in sculpture these forms and the process of development returned to mind both consciously and unconsciously. One thinks an idea is discarded and used up but one never knows quite where it is going to end up and whether it will come back and if so, in what form. In this case these ideas of memory and loss (the Tempieto was built as a martyrium for St. Peter who was supposedly executed on that site) emerged in the form of this beautiful little building, which in many ways, represented a quantum leap in my mind. It was the genesis of a new tear in the universe, containing references to its historical past as well as becoming the model for the architecture of the future. While I have no control over the influence of my work, I sometimes comfort myself with the thought that I might just put out an idea, or the trace of an idea, and there is no predicting what will happen to it. Through thousands of years ideas are not at rest, and they often get picked up unknowingly, unconsciously. That may be all one can ask for as an artist or a thinker.

In later works I returned to and reinterpreted ideas that started in the 1970s, for example, the notion of the circle or circles-within-circles. And when I finally saw the Tempieto, it was encased in scaffolding—hardly the pure Renaissance form I had expected. *Explanation, An. Of Spring and the Weight of Air* is really a tribute to the Tempietto—but it is also influenced by hot air balloons, amusement park rides, and disasters like Three Mile Island.

[4–5] *opposite*

ALICE AYCOCK,
*THE HUNDRED SMALL
ROOMS*, LAUMEIER
SCULPTURE PARK,
SAINT LOUIS, MISSOURI,
1984–1986.
[ROBERT PETTUS]

[4–6]

ALICE AYCOCK,
WORLD TRADE CENTER
PROPOSAL, 2001.
COMPUTER SIMULATION.
[ALICE AYCOCK]

[4–7]

ALICE AYCOCK,
*COLLECTED GHOST
STORIES FROM THE
WORKHOUSE, FROM
THE SERIES HOW TO
CATCH AND MANU-
FACTURE GHOSTS*,
1980.
[ALICE AYCOCK]

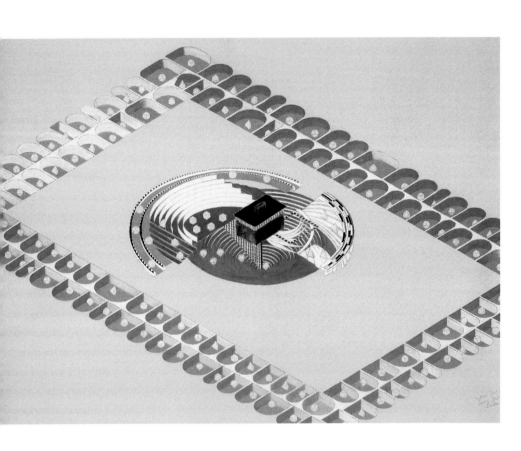

A series of drawings made in the mid-1980s explored different sorts of places that were supposedly sacred, holy, or mysterious, and I configured these places as a series of board games [4–8]. A lot of these works were, in a sense, palimpsests. When I begin a work, I have to start somewhere, there has to be something to begin with, some image, some drawings—which I can work over, erase, and build on. I rarely start by just thinking about something that came from nowhere; for me, it always comes from somewhere, somewhere else. I need something else to start my creative engine.

There are works in which the machine has just gotten loose pure and simple: The walls of the circular section of *The Machine that Makes the World* are on wheels and the viewer actually moves through a series of steel gates into the center of the work and is turned into and back out of the work [4–9]. On the walls are statements that talk about amusement parks, stockyards, prisons, institutions, and insane asylums. Other works are about the notion of a whirlwind and something spinning, either chaotically or not. One piece has two identical circular vortexes—each about 10 feet in diameter—that begin to spin. They whirl themselves up like the amusement park ride that goes vertically into the air. When you are looking into the room with the art, it feels like being next to a jet engine. Another piece, *The Thousand and One Nights in the Mansion of Bliss*, attempts to create some sort of generic image that suggests the history of tool making from arrowhead blades to windmills to turbines to Cuisinarts [4–10]. It spins very slowly and seductively. It's somewhat terrifying; it's also kind of marvelous.

Through the 1980s I made a number of works that drew upon amusement park architecture, the super-duper-looper, and how it relates to the highway forms. My interest in highways began with my master's thesis, which discussed the American highway system as a vast construction comparable to Neolithic earthworks. The vast system that I wrote about in the late 1960s and early 1970s has become a cancerous system that has eaten up everything in its way. But at that time I was interested in the highway as a phenomenological labyrinth and the amusement park ride like the super-duper-looper as its American metaphorical counterpart. It became the basis for much of my art [4–11].

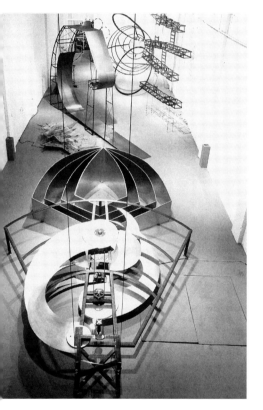

[4-11]
ALICE AYCOCK,
*GHOST BALLET FOR
THE EAST BANK
MACHINEWORKS*,
NASHVILLE, TENNESSEE,
2005–2007.
[GARY LAYDA]

East River Roundabout is located on the East River in New York, installed on the roof of an old building recycled as a park pavilion. The immediate surroundings are very urban and gritty and intense—the FDR, the Queensborough Bridge, the Roosevelt Island Tram. Another work was constructed based on a diagram of the mating rituals of hummingbirds and their movements when they hovered in the air—the site was a government building in Baltimore. When you see it on the plaza it looks like something from outer space has landed and is taking over the building.

Waltzing Matilda, created in the mid-1990s, involved this fantasy person who wanted to dance through history. Somehow she thought that using a spinning top with a draw-ing point on the end and large big steel plate cut with the patterns of certain dances—baroque dances, contra dances— would help her achieve that ambition. Her idea was that if you could recreate this movement from a particular time, perhaps you could return to that time, as if in a time machine. There is a long story associated with her fantasy and I wrote it as a play. Surrounding the installation are numerous drawings. And I have always liked the idea: "What if you could play a marble game with the stars?" I remember reading somewhere that perhaps the universe is really just a child playing a game of marbles. I thought about how people have looked up at the stars throughout history and how they envision themselves, how they fantasize themselves, how they create themselves. So I played this game with stars, using different systems drawn from history. In addition to dances from different eras, there are also languages from different times in history, games, mechanical movements—I certainly couldn't leave that one out because at one point the universe was supposed to move mechanically, like a clock—cities and war diagrams that have been drawn into the starry night. They are all diagrams, and I love diagrams, because I can dream into them. I can imagine schemes for the sculptural constructs. Years ago, I set up a stationary camera—with black-and-white film—and I snapped pictures as the clouds moved in and out of the frame. The project concerned the transitory nature of things and the idea that things are always in transition; I believed that then [4–12]. But in response I made a body of work which in a sense was trying to stop change, to hold it back. Then several years ago, I thought about what sort of piece I would make if I were able to accept the fact that nothing lasts forever. All things turn to dust; I would really like to make a piece about the transitory nature of life, of cultures, of societies, of artists, of my own ego, all the things I may do, or may not get to do, or wanted to do. I still want to make that piece [4–13].

*ADAPTED BY
MARC TREIB
FROM A LECTURE
BY ALICE AYCOCK
PRESENTED AT
THE SYMPOSIUM
"SPATIAL RECALL:
THE PLACE OF MEMORY
IN ARCHITECTURE
AND LANDSCAPE,"
HELD AT THE
UNIVERSITY OF
CALIFORNIA, BERKELEY,
ON 10 MARCH 2007.*

[4-12]
ALICE AYCOCK,
SAND/FANS, 1971,
RECREATED AT THE
JAMES SALOMON
CONTEMPORARY
WAREHOUSE, 2008.
[TIM LEE]

[4-13]
ALICE AYCOCK,
UNTITLED PROPOSAL
TITLED LEAP OF FAITH,
2001.
COMPUTER SIMULATION.
[ALICE AYCOCK]

5

Rivers, Meanders, and Memory

Matt Kondolf

INTRODUCTION

We may say that rivers have distinct personalities: forms and habits determined by their geologic setting, their flow regime—those seasonal and year-to-year patterns of floods and dry-season low flows—and their sediment load, that is, how much mud, sand, or gravel they transport. Rivers are naturally dynamic, changing in response to wet years and dry, the seasons, the odd landslide, and even the trees that fall in the channel. As Heraclitus said: "You cannot step in the same river twice, because the second time it is not the same river." Rivers are part of a larger landscape, veins in a network that carries water, sediment, and wood, and through which fish migrate—most famously, salmon to their natal spawning grounds.

Rivers have long histories and their current forms reflect not only present forces but also the legacy of past. Traumatic events such as deforestation and massive flooding can cause the river to adopt a new channel, to re-occupy an old one, or to utterly change character. More subtly, changes in the supply of water and sediment from the watershed to the river can continue to influence river processes and form for decades. Building subdivisions in the uplands, converting forest to agriculture, building dams, or leveeing-off floodplains can all change the independent variables that influence river behavior. Even when the event itself is no longer legible, its influence may persist. For this reason we say that rivers have memories.

Agriculture was hard on the lands of the eastern seaboard of the United States in the nineteenth century. Farming practices not only exhausted nutrients from the soil, but plowing without regard to slope led to massive soil erosion and the transfer of sediment from upland fields to the banks of small streams and river floodplains—where it is easily eroded by the modern river.[1] These factors explain why the load of suspended sediment carried by these rivers did not decline in the twentieth century despite soil conservation practices and the dramatic reductions in upland erosion rates. Thus, the legacy of sediment from nineteenth-century land management still contributes to the making of present-day rivers, the persistent influence of a traumatic memory.

Humans routinely alter rivers for convenience, but rivers remember their true nature and when the time is right, they

[5-1]

GREEN RIVER, WYOMING.

[MATT KONDOLF, 1982]

A FORMER MEANDER BEND OF THE UPPER PART OF THE RIVER— NOW LARGELY FILLED WITH SEDIMENT BUT RETAINING DISTINCTIVE SOIL CHARACTERISTICS AND HYDROLOGY— AND CONSEQUENTLY SUPPORTING DIFFERENT VEGETATION THAN THE ADJACENT UPLANDS.

may reassert it. Viewing the land from above we can see the traces of former river channels, such as meander bends long ago filled with sediment but still reflecting different soil conditions and vegetation [5–1]. To allow the straightening of a busy county road alongside it, the Carmel River in California was also straightened in the 1960s. The engineers cut off a meander bend to the north and lined the margin of the new, straight river with rock. Since that work was completed the river developed a "sympathetic" meander bend to the south to compensate for its lost sinuosity [5–2]. The Walla Walla River in Washington was also artificially straightened, but it too did not forget its meandering pattern and in subsequent floods reasserted its original course [5–3].

THE MEMORY OF RIVERS IN THE CITY

Humans have settled along rivers for reasons of transport, power, water supply, fishing, and the availability of level fertile lands. Although in developed countries other sources of transport, power, and even water supply have largely supplanted their utilitarian value, rivers still exert a strong pull on the human psyche, as evidenced by the strength of the urban waterfront renewal in numerous cities.[2]

[5–2]
CARMEL RIVER, CALIFORNIA. OBLIQUE AERIAL VIEW SOUTHWARD.
[MATT KONDOLF, 1983]

IN THE 1960s THE COUNTY'S PUBLIC WORKS DEPARTMENT CUT OFF A NORTHWARD BEND (BOTTOM OF PHOTO) WHILE STRAIGHTENING THE ADJACENT ROAD. SUBSEQUENTLY, A "SYMPATHETIC" MEANDER BEND DEVELOPED TOWARDS THE SOUTH TO COMPENSATE FOR LOSS OF SINUOSITY.

[5-3]

WALLA WALLA RIVER,
OREGON.
OBLIQUE AERIAL VIEW.
[US ARMY CORPS OF
ENGINEERS]

THE RIVER AFTER THE
1965 FLOOD, WHEN
THE RIVER BROKE
OUT OF ITS LEVEES
AND REASSERTED ITS
FORMER MEANDERING
PATTERN.

As cities have urbanized, the smaller creeks have been buried in underground culverts and are largely forgotten—that is, until the culverts begin to fail and we are reminded that there are creeks beneath them. Buried rivers in London and Philadelphia, for example, are still evident in their urban form.[3] In Berkeley, California, most of the creeks were buried in the twentieth century, but sensing their loss, a local creek group has stenciled patterns on curbs to show the underground course of buried streams in the city—a way of retaining the memory of these lost waterways. And in recent years it has become increasingly more common to "daylight" these buried creeks and restore them as free-flowing surface channels [5–4]. In addition to breaking up and removing the concrete pipes that had contained the streams, daylighting projects may involve varying degrees of channel design and development of adjacent parks or commercial areas.

Given the close historical dependence of cities on rivers it is not surprising that the basic forms of many cities have been inherited from the fluvial landforms upon which they were built. The city of Wasserburg, Bavaria, was built on a point bar of the River Inn. Meander bends typically have an

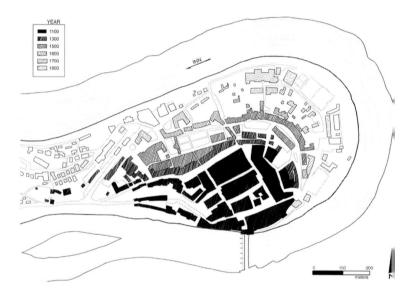

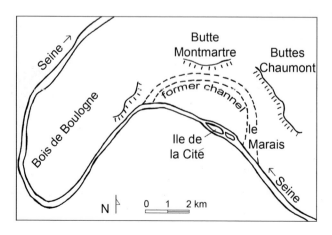

[5-4]

STRAWBERRY CREEK,
BERKELEY, CALIFORNIA.
THE REACH OF THE
CREEK, FORMERLY
BURIED IN A
CONCRETE PIPE,
AFTER "DAYLIGHTING."
[MATT KONDOLF, 1990]

[5-5]

WASSERBURG, GERMANY.
[ADAPTED FROM
FLUESSE UND BÄCHE,
ERHALTEN-ENTWICKELN-
GESTALTEN, WASSER-
WIRTSCHAFT IN BAYERN,
1989, COURTESY OF
WALTER BINDER]

THE URBAN FORM OF
WASSERBURG REFLECTS
THE HISTORY OF ITS
GROWTH ON AN
ACCRETING POINT BAR.
THE CONSTRUCTION
OF NEW BUILDINGS
EXPANDED OUTWARDS
IN CONCENTRIC BANDS
AS THE CHANNEL
MIGRATED AWAY FROM
THE CITY AND THE
POINT BAR GREW.

[5-6]

PARIS, FRANCE.
[ADAPTED FROM "THE
SITE AND GROWTH OF
PARIS," THE GEOGRAPH-
ICAL JOURNAL, 1941]

PHYSIOGRAPHIC FEATURES
UNDERLYING THE URBAN
FORM. THE HILL OF
MONTMARTE, AFFORDING
SUPERB VIEWS OVER THE
CITY, IS SIMPLY THE HIGH,
OUTSIDE BANK OF A
FORMER MEANDER
BEND OF THE SEINE.

eroding, high bank on the outer edge of the bend, with a lower point bar forming as the channel migrates across its floodplain. As the outside bank eroded, and the point bar grew into the former channel, Wasserburg grew outward on the newly created land, resulting in bands of urban growth each younger than the one before [5–5]. In the early twentieth century, engineers placed rock at the base of the eroding bank, halting the migrating of the River Inn—but the basic urban form remains a legacy of the river process. Like Wasserburg the urban form of Paris clearly reflects its fluvial heritage. The basic pattern of its boulevards were inherited from historical city walls, but these, in turn, had been built parallel to the course of the river along which the city was constructed. The Marais district was a swamp (*marais*), part of a former channel of the river, and the striking relief of the hill of Montmarte derives from a high bank at the outside of an ancient meander bend of which the Buttes Chaumont were also a part [5–6]. The Seine has long since migrated southwestward from this bank, leaving behind one of the city's most striking physical features, another example of urban form inherited from the river along which the city developed.

When we look at a river, we are inclined to accept it as it is, as if it had always been this way. But what looks like a pristine, natural form may be an artifact of profound changes wrought by human agents. Along the Eygues River, a pre-Alpine tributary to the Rhône River in southeastern France, the riparian forest has been designated by the European Union as a site of ecological interest under the Natura 2000 program. Stemming from this classification, the river has been granted priority for the completion of its preservation, and has been named as a reference site for studying the restoration of degraded systems. In actual fact, the riparian forest so treasured today is an artifact of twentieth-century landscape changes. In the nineteenth century, the rural population density was several times greater than it is today, both in the mountains (where wood cutting and sheep grazing devegetated and destabilized slopes, leading to high rates of sediment delivery to the river) and along the river banks (where virtually every square meter was put to use: for orchard, cultivated land, pasture, or *oseraie*, willow thickets cut annually to yield material for baskets and vineyards) [5–7, 5–8]. The Industrial Revolution triggered a migration from rural to urban areas that reduced human pressure on the catchment and allowed the forests to return to the slopes. Consequently, erosion and sediment delivery to the channel declined, a process accelerated by a further reduction in sheep grazing after World War II.[4] The wide, dynamic, unvegetated sand-and-gravel river channel of the early nineteenth century—typically about 350m wide and well-documented on the Napoleonic cadastral maps— had narrowed to half that width by the late twentieth century. As the channel narrowed, willows, poplars, and alders took hold in the former channel area, creating the riparian forest so

[5–7] *opposite*

LOWER EYGUES RIVER, FRANCE.

[MATT KONDOLF, 2008]

THE DENSE RIPARIAN CORRIDOR IN THE COMMUNE OF VINSOBRES SEEN FROM THE CONFLUENCE OF LE RIEU, A NORTH-BANK TRIBUTARY, 5 KILOMETERS DOWNSTREAM FROM NYONS. ALL OF RIPARIAN VEGETATION SHOWN IN THIS VIEW DEVELOPED SINCE THE NINETEENTH CENTURY.

[5–8] *below*

LOWER EYGUES RIVER, FRANCE.

[KONDOLF, PIÉGAY, AND LANDON. "CHANGES SINCE 1830 IN THE RIPARIAN ZONE OF THE LOWER EYGUES RIVER, FRANCE," *LANDSCAPE ECOLOGY*, 2007]

INTENSIVE LAND-USE ALONG THE RIVER IN THE COMMUNE OF VINSOBRES, FRANCE, DOCUMENTED BY THE NAPOLEONIC CADASTRAL MAP OF 1830. THE DETAIL SHOWS THE CONFLUENCE OF THE TRIBUTARY, LE RIEU, COVERING THE AREA SHOWN IN 5–7. LAND-USE TYPES BY PARCEL ARE SUPERIMPOSED ON SCREENED VERSION OF THE 1830 VINSOBRES CADASTRAL MAP FROM THE ARCHIVES DÉPARTEMENTALES DE LA DRÔME, VALENCE.

ecologically valued today. Ironically, the officials who designated this channel as an ecological reference site were almost certainly unaware of its nineteenth-century form, a landscape memory largely forgotten by the current inhabitants but nonetheless shaping the present environment.

RIVER RESTORATION AND MEMORY

With the improvement in water quality since the implementation in the United States of the Clean Water Act—with comparable legislation in other countries—river restoration has become increasingly common in the developed world. Through 2004, in the U.S. alone, there were over 37,000 documented projects undertaken at a cost of over $17 billion.[5] Of these, three-quarters are in Pacific coastal drainages, reflecting the magnitude of efforts to restore habitats for the Pacific salmon now threatened with extinction.

The habitat values of freshwater river channels depend in large part on their renewal by dynamic fluvial processes. For example, as meander bends migrate, concentrated flow along the eroding outer bend creates deep pools; trees fall into the channel increasing complexity and providing cover for fish; gravel deposits provide sites for spawning; and sloughs and

side channels provide shallow-water habitat for juvenile fish. Migrating salmon remember their natal streams and return to exploit these habitats for spawning and rearing. Where dynamic processes are stifled—as below large dams that control flows and trap sediment supply from upstream, or where riverbanks are stabilized by rock walls—fish habitat degrades. Fine sediment collects in stream gravels without being scoured by floods, a simplified channel develops form losing the nooks and crannies needed by fish—and the proportion of invasive exotic fish increases at the expense of native species. A growing body of scientific literature indicates that dynamic, actively migrating channels provide the best ecological habitats, and that ecological value diminishes with decreased flow and channel dynamics.[6] Thus, where feasible, the most effective long-term restoration strategy would be to restore fluvial processes. This, in turn, will maintain the habitats needed by salmon and other species.[7]

Interestingly, one of the most popular river restoration approaches in the United States uses a form-based classification to determine the "proper" form for a given section of a river and to construct a single channel whose correct shape and dimensions will produce a stable form. (This approach implicitly assumes that stability is desirable, however, despite evidence that dynamic channels are more valuable ecologically.) This method involves inventorying and classifying stream "types" according to the Rosgen classification system, selecting structures suitable for stream types, and then reconstructing the channel according to this ideal form.[8] In projects so designed, large boulders and the butt ends of trees typically stabilize the outsides of the meander bends, and include boulder structures within the bed—even in channels composed of smaller sediment where boulders would not naturally occur.

Despite criticism from the scientific community, this approach has proved popular with managers because they can quickly train staff and begin undertaking projects using a step-by-step "cookbook" approach without the long delays that a real scientific study might entail.[9] The classification system typically specifies a single, stable meandering channel as the "proper" geometry for a given site. The popularity of these single-thread meandering channels reflects an unrecognized but profound cultural preference for such forms, a shared cultural memory of such channel forms in Atlantic-climate northern Europe. When this northern European aesthetic is imposed on a dynamic, Mediterranean-climate river, the results are not always successful.

A very imageable example of this preference is evident in a channel reconstruction project on Uvas Creek, in Gilroy, California. Completed in November 1995, the channel was a typical Rosgen-type restoration project, with symmetrical meanders, its outside bends protected by logs and boulders, with rock weirs across the channel [5–9A]. In all, the restoration resembled the meandering channels common in the pastoral landscapes of northern Europe. The design—and fate—of these efforts were essentially identical to a dozen such projects in northern and central California in the 1990s. Three months after its completion, the "restoration" washed out in a modest flood: Uvas Creek cut across the constructed floodplain and, in effect, ignored and abandoned the structures designed to lock the channel in its designed bends [5–9B]. When we examine the restoration plan for the project, we find that the designers believed: "The channel was once a stable C4 channel;" here, they referred to an alpha-numeric designation under the Rosgen classification system for a single-thread meandering channel. However, nineteenth-century maps and early aerial photographs suggest otherwise. They show a multi-thread, braided channel typical of streams draining the California Coast Range, reflecting with its episodic Mediterranean-climate rainfall and runoff, and high sediment loads.[10] While less appealing than the tidy meandering channel, such a scruffy channel better reflects the dynamic conditions prevailing in this environment. In effect, the river remembered its true nature and rebelled against the imposed form derived from an idealized cultural memory.

The cultural preference for meandering channels is reflected in the work of eighteenth-century theorists of beauty such as the English artist William Hogarth, who believed that:

> The eye hath this sort of enjoyment in ... serpentine rivers whose forms ... are composed principally of what I call the waving and serpentine lines ... that leads the eye in a wanton kind of chase, and from the pleasure that give the mind, entitles it to the name of beautiful.[11]

Such notions were put into practice by eighteenth-century English landscape designers such as Capability Brown, who constructed serpentine channels on the estates of his clients, and continued in the nineteenth century in road designs by Frederick Law Olmsted.[12] Landscape and psychological research suggest that curved streets are preferred over straight ones because of the anticipation of what lies around the corner.[13] More broadly, "deflected vistas" (be they valleys, paths, or rivers) are preferred.[14] The serpentine line has been used in more than one advertisement for sport utility vehicles, most

[5–9A]

UVAS CREEK, GILROY, CALIFORNIA. VIEWED DOWNSTREAM FROM THE SANTA TERESA BOULEVARD BRIDGE IN JANUARY 1996, TWO MONTHS AFTER THE CONSTRUCTION OF A CHANNEL RECONSTRUCTION PROJECT. [COURTESY OF THE CITY OF GILROY]

THE SYMMETRICAL MEANDERS, WITH THE OUTSIDE BANKS PROTECTED BY BOULDERS AND LOG REVETMENTS, ARE TYPICAL OF THESE PROJECTS.

THE SAME VIEW AFTER A MODEST FLOOD WASHED THE RECON- STRUCTION PROJECT OUT IN FEBRUARY 1996 (RETURN INTERVAL OF ABOUT SIX YEARS). UVAS CREEK IGNORED THE CONSTRUCTED MEANDER BENDS AND REVETMENTS, CUTTING DIRECTLY ACROSS THE MEANDER BENDS AND REESTABLISHING A FORM MORE TYPICAL FOR ITS DYNAMIC MEDITERRANEAN- CLIMATE SETTING: A WIDE, UNVEGETATED SAND-AND-GRAVEL BED, IN VEGETATION WILL ESTABLISH IN BETWEEN FLOODS, ONLY TO BE SCOURED IN SUBSEQUENT FLOODS.

notably a recent ad for Jeep Cherokee that featured a sinuously-bending highway that transitioned into a meandering river [5–10]. This aesthetic preference for the single meandering channel, given continued cultural reinforcement, may counter scientific reasoning, however, as we have seen.

CONCLUSION

Our landscape is shaped by rivers and memory. The form of our cities, built along rivers, reflects the fluvial processes that have shaped those alluvial landscapes. The streams buried in the course of urbanization and largely forgotten, increasingly reassert themselves as their culverts leak and collapse. As we remember these hidden veins of the landscape, more and more we seek to restore them to their rightful place on the surface. Just as the salmon returns to her natal stream to spawn, we find our society drawn to restore rivers and streams. While the instinct is essentially healthy, we see many projects that seek to rebuild river channels in the image of meanders from a pastoral landscape of our collective cultural memory from northern European landscapes. These efforts often fail because the projects are realized in landscapes where such idealized forms had never existed in nature. In these cases, the river usually remembers and reasserts its true nature, which is often more dynamic and messy than the imposed, idealized form given it by its human engineers.

[5–10]
ADVERTISEMENTS FOR
JEEP SPORT-UTILITY
VEHICLE.

NOTES
I thank Kristen Podolak for extensive help in manuscript and figure preparation. Jen Natali prepared the map of Wasserburg, and Walter Binder gave permission to adapt from the original figure. Marc Treib provided insightful review comments.

1 R. H. Meade and S. W. Trimble, "Changes in Sediment Loads in Rivers of the Atlantic Drainage of the United States since 1900," *Effects of Man on the Interface of the Hydrological Cycle with the Physical Environment*, International Association of Hydrological Sciences Publication 113, 1974, pp. 99–104.

2 B. Otto, K. McCormick, and M. Leccese, *Ecological Riverfront Design: Restoring Rivers, Connecting Communities*, American Planning Association, Planning Advisory Service Report Number 518–519, 2004.

3 N. J. Barton, *The Lost Rivers of London*, London: Phoenix House, 1962; Anne Winston Spirn, *The Language of Landscape*, New Haven: Yale University Press, 1998.

4 G. M. Kondolf, H. Piégay, and N. Landon, "Changes Since 1830 in the Riparian Zone of the Lower Eygues River, France," *Landscape Ecology* 22, 2007, pp. 367–384; A. Brookes and F. D. Shield, eds, *River Channel Restoration*, Chichester: John Wiley, 1996; P. W. Downs, K. S. Skinner, and G. M. Kondolf, "Rivers and Streams," *Handbook of Ecological Restoration* 11, 2001, pp. 267–291.

5 E. S. Bernhardt, M. A. Palmer, J. D. Allan, G. Alexander, K. Barnes, S. Brooks, J. Carr, S. Clayton, C. Dahm, J. Follsted-Shah, D. Galat, S. Gloss, P. Goodwin, D. Hart, B. Hassett, R. Jenkinson, S. Katz, G. M. Kondolf, P. S. Lake, R. Lave, J. L. Meyer, T. K. O'Donnell, L. Pagano, B. Powell, and E. Sudduth, "Synthesizing U.S. River Restoration Efforts," *Science* 308, 2005, pp. 636–637.

6 J. V. Ward and J. A. Stanford, "Ecological Connectivity in Alluvial River Ecosystems and its Disruption by Flow Regulation," *Regulated Rivers Research and Management* 11, 1995, 105–119.

7 E. Wohl, P. L. Angermeier, B. Bledsoe, G. M. Kondolf, L. MacDonnell, D. M. Merritt, M. A. Palmer, N. L. Poff, and D. Tarboton, "River Restoration," *Water Resources Research* 41, 2005, W10301, doi:10.1029/2005WR003985; G. M. Kondolf, A. Boulton, S. O'Daniel, G. Poole, F. Rahel, E. Stanley, E. Wohl, A. Bang, J. Carlstrom, C. Cristoni, H. Huber, S. Koljonen, P. Louhi, and K. Nakamura, "Process-based Ecological River Restoration: Visualizing Three-dimensional Connectivity and Dynamic Vectors to Recover Lost Linkages," *Ecology and Society*. vol. 11 (2), 2006, [online]: http://www.ecologyandsociety.org/vol11/iss2/art5/

8 D. L. Rosgen, "A Classification of Natural Rivers," *Catena* 22, 1994, pp. 169–199: D. L. Rosgen and B. L. Fittante, "Fish Habitat Structures: A Selection Guide Using Stream Classification," *5th Trout Stream Improvement Workshop*. Lock Haven University, Lock Haven, Pennsylvania, 1986.

9 J. R. Miller and J. B. Ritter, "An Examination of the Rosgen Classification of Natural Rivers," *Catena* 27, 1996, 295–299; M. W. Doyle, D. E. Miller, and J. M. Harbor, "Should River Restoration Be Based on Classification Schemes or Process Models? Insights from the History of Geomorphology," in *Proceedings of the ASCE International Conference on Water Resources Engineering*, Seattle, 1999; K. E. Juracek and F. A. Fitzpatrick, "Limitations and Implications of Stream Classification," *Journal of the American Water Resources Assn* 39, 2003, pp. 659–670; A. Simon, M. Doyle, M. Kondolf, F. D. Shields Jr., B. Rhoads, and M. McPhillips, "Critical Evaluation of How the Rosgen Classification and Associated 'Natural Channel Design' Methods Fail to Integrate and Quantify Fluvial Processes and Channel Response," *Journal of the American Water Resources Association* 43: 5, 2007, pp. 1–15; D. Malakoff, "The River Doctor," *Science* 305, 2004, pp. 937–939.

10 G. M. Kondolf, M. W. Smeltzer, and S. Railsback, "Design and Performance of a Channel Reconstruction Project in a Coastal California Gravel-bed Stream," *Environmental Management* 28(6), 2001, pp. 761–776.

11 William Hogarth, *Analysis of Beauty*, London: Heath Edition, 1753, p. 33.

12 M. E. Myers, "The Line of Grace: Principles of Road Aesthetics in the Design of the Blue Ridge Parkway," *Landscape Journal* 23, 2004, pp. 121–140.

13 Gordon Cullen, *Townscape*, London: Architectural Press, 1961.

14 Jay Appleton, *The Experience of Landscape*, London: John Wiley, 1975.

6

Displacements: Canals, Rivers, and Flows

Georges Descombes

The projects I will discuss below are rooted, for the most part, in the territory—Swiss and French—where I was born, have lived, and have worked. The Mexican novelist Carlos Fuentes once wrote that we have to imagine the past and recall the future. In that sense, I will imagine these river and other projects and perhaps recall their future—one is still in construction and will require a long period of time for its completion. But to establish a gateway into my way of thinking and approach to design I will present one element of a larger park, a "tunnel bridge" made about two decades ago.

L'AIRE AND LANCY

Any sketch is both a contemporary record and an interpretation of a historical situation [6–1].

The drawings of the landscape I made in preparation for our interventions to the River Aire, on the outskirts of Geneva, record and interpret the changes in the territory that have transpired over the years. Some drawings depict a landscape that could have existed a hundred years earlier; others describe the present state of the things, but in a biased way that makes the changes more evident.

This territory is also filled with projects left realized but which remain nevertheless instructive. As part of our research we consulted the municipal archives, and there we found other projects to control the river, including one proposed in the late nineteenth century [6–2]. That drawing traced the full course of the river; it measured almost ten feet in length. (I think I was the first person to look at the map since its production a hundred years ago.) The drawing was beautifully rendered in ink and watercolor on heavy paper. It depicted the project for a canal superimposed over a plan showing several kilometers of the existing river; they were accompanied by a series of 135 transverse sections made over a period of years. From those sections we learned that in one year around 1880 the river shifted its course almost 50 meters. No river is stable; each river has its own life. In the 1930s the change in agricultural methods to increase production also affected the land along the river; to effect this change in method about 400 kilometers of agricultural drainage were built. The existing river was then cut short by a long canal, portions of which are

[6–1]

GEORGES DESCOMBES,
THE LANDSCAPE OF
THE RIVER AIRE VALLEY,
NEAR GENEVA,
SWITZERLAND. 1978.
INK SKETCH.
[GEORGES DESCOMBES]

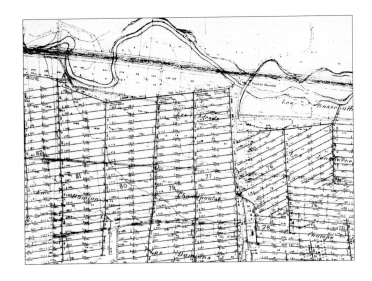

attributed to the noted Swiss engineer Robert Maillart. Water
flowed rapidly through the concrete linings of the channel and
passed any floods to neighboring communities downstream.

Almost ten years ago a competition was held to "restore"
the river to a more natural state. This river is a part of the
territory of my childhood; there is a lot of history here and a
great number of stories told between friends. My father was a
bookseller, which as a child gave me access—at least in writing
—to the American landscapes described by the novelists
James Fennimore Cooper, James Oliver Curwood, or Joseph
Conrad. So with these impressions in my mind I used to go
to the river with my dog, excitedly expecting to encounter
a grizzly bear or something walking or fighting in the snow.
The land and its trees and river then seemed large and the
reality of my own dimensions small. That has all changed,
of course. The dimensions have changed. I became taller and
the landscape smaller.

I had sketched the canal many times long before—
possibly 20 years before [see 6–1]. Now the organizers of the
competition asked me to demolish the canal and to make
something new; to re-install a new river where the old one had
once been. That was the task set by the program; or perhaps it
was just the dream of the organizers. But before discussing the
nature of our proposal, let me present an earlier project at the
Parc de Lancy.

This park is located on the edge of Geneva, the city in which I live. As a result of the extensive transformation of the River Aire's watershed, a road was built on the site of the future park in the 1940s. The result of that construction devastated a rivulet that until that time had flowed freely in a small valley. Instead of building a bridge—the traditional and perfect way of straddling a stream—the authorities had substituted what we might call a "landslide" approach based on imperfect logic regarding drainage and sanitation. In the process the little valley disappeared—blocked—and the stream ended up in a culvert.

In the first phase of design, completed in 1981, we addressed the problems created by filling the small vale. To preserve safe access to the new public park, the authorities requested a pedestrian underpass set beneath the road then in the process of being widened. The two access points for the crossing—one on either side of the stream—differed in their conditions and created an ambiguous situation. Crossing through the embankment suggested a tunnel; crossing the stream suggested a bridge. This was a conceptually heavy load for such a small passage. The architectural device we proposed was based on this conceptual duality. It preserved both elements—bridge and tunnel—within a complex system that attempts to answer the brief directly, while at the same time revealing the existing site conditions [6–3]. The design refers to the history of the place and its successive transformations, and in doing so, it witnesses the upheavals experienced by

[6–2]
MAP OF THE RIVER
AIRE WATERSHED
[DETAIL],
NEAR GENEVA,
SWITZERLAND,
NINETEENTH CENTURY.
[MUNICIPAL ARCHIVES,
CITY OF GENEVA]

the place—and questioned its current state of confusion. It therefore maintains a status as "lost property," slightly detached from the place to which it is nevertheless connected. The "tunnel-bridge" is a tube of a corrugated steel sections some 30 meters long and 3 meters in diameter, bolted together in situ. A 96-meter-long footbridge ran the length of the tube and extended beyond it on both ends. The choice of an elementary geometry—circle and line—as well as the use of steel, aims at giving the device a tension that clearly affirms the design as a contemporary intervention devoid of nostalgia. By putting the bridge in the tunnel we offered a composite solution while still revealing the nature of the problem. This composite form also grants an air of discovery and adventure to what is normally a rather mundane act.

The River Aire flows southward from Geneva, through valleys historically devoted to farming. In the nineteenth century the river was incrementally reconfigured as a canal to control flooding. The process continued during the Depression to provide employment, and the final segment of the canal was completed only after World War II. In 2001 the authorities decided to "restore" the river to its "original" form, and an invited competition requested ideas for realizing the restoration.

[6–3]
GEORGES DESCOMBES, PARC DE LANCY, GENEVA, SWITZERLAND, 1981. PHOTO-COLLAGE SHOWING THE TUNNEL-BRIDGE FROM ABOVE. [JACQUES BERTHET]

There was no way we could accept the suggested approach, however. For one, the environmental conditions surrounding the Aire had changed drastically since the nineteenth century. What had once been farmland was now partly suburban development. In addition, the construction of housing had displaced and paved considerable amounts of land—which meant the risk for flooding was now greater than ever before. Most important, however, was our belief that the canal—as a canal—was an important part of the heritage and cultural landscape of Geneva and that it should be maintained in some form as a memory of the city's and region's history. We also believed that engaging memory and history when designing should not be replaying the past. As the geographer André Corboz told us: "Memory is the study of the legible traces left on the terrain of intervention ... Memory is the legitimate exercise of cultural imagination."

After winning the competition, I spent almost five years reading all the books and documents I could locate that tracked the shifting dimensions and history of the river and the canal. Of course, no matter what we do the river will continue to flow. But today there is a quite complex landscape and social situation, with agricultural fields on one side and housing on the other—as well as intensive uses for leisure along the river

[6–4]
GEORGES DESCOMBES,
THE RIVER AIRE
PROJECT,
NEAR GENEVA,
SWITZERLAND, 2001.
CONCEPT SKETCH.
[GEORGES DESCOMBES]

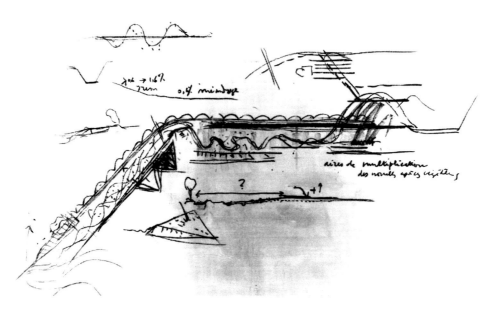

banks, and on and in the river itself. After completing our
research we determined that this kind of a project has three
components [6–4]. We can't avoid maintaining the agricultural
uses—their retention was a sensible requirement. Neither
can we get rid of the people living there by simply saying:
"Well, this area is now a nature preserve." For some time
now the land along the river has been a park system—and a
rather precious one at that. It has been classified as a "rural
public space," a concept first proposed in the 1930s by Maurice
Braillard, then head of the Public Works Department for the
city of Geneva. There was also the issue of water remediation
which was, in fact, the main reason for holding the competition
in the first place. So you have three components to be considered: agriculture, public access to the river and leisure uses,
and the river's own ecological improvement.

The total length of canalized river governed by the
competition is about 5 kilometers. We were asked to study the
entire length of the project area, but at the same time to design
in greater detail an experimental segment to be realized within
the first few months of design. This first segment tested the
possibilities for the larger site, the conditions for its realization,
and not least of all, examined the benefits and difficulties
arising from coordinating a quite large group of consultants—
landscape architects, biologists, civil and hydraulic engineers

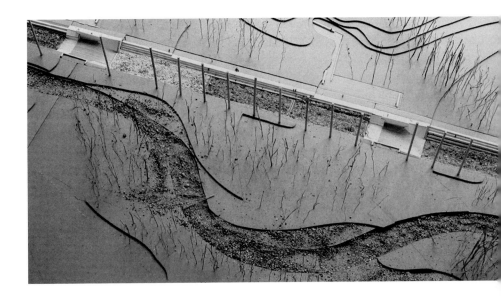

—each with their own vocabulary. The experience proved to be very useful, however, and we are currently re-evaluating this early stage of the project to correct it—or reintroduce it —in our work in the future.

This first part of the canal, with its double-curve, would be returned to its form as a river with natural banks [6–5]. The softened shoreline will encourage an interaction between the water and the banks that will support the restoration of natural systems of flows and vegetation. The straight part of the canal, in contrast, will become a kind of boulevard that on one side buffers the land from the water. The canal thus represents an "in between" condition, in some ways like a battle zone: with land for leisure uses and housing, the former canal, the new river meanders, and the agricultural fields. The remnants of the canal's concrete walls and floor will provide comfort-able places to walk and they will guide visitors; they will take form, in part, as a field of gardens that extends for some five kilometers. Fill will reduce the existing depth of the water—now three meters—by half. Along the new 15-meter-wide promenade an open channel will collect the drainage from the left bank, using it to develop a series of wetlands set 400 meters apart.

We will reconstruct the landscape using water, organizing the river—beginning with its total length, but ultimately arriving at all the little veins that feed it. Where the land is wet, we will install platforms. Of course, the river also represents a watershed, so when restoring the river, you must restore all the territory around it. It isn't one line of water that you restore; it's a complete system. As a result, we have also had to make suggestions for organizing public activity far from the river, to lower the public's pressure on the new river. It has been a kind of dance between the river and the public, which has necessitated a strong didactic aspect to this project. In many ways we are hoping to find new relationships between the river, the surrounding landscape, the inhabitants, and the farmers. And because of this we have spent considerable time in public meetings and making exhibitions and explanatory publications. The project has already been under construction for several years and will take more time to complete. Projects like this cannot be rushed.

[6–5]

GEORGES DESCOMBES WITH ADR, THE RIVER AIRE PROJECT, NEAR GENEVA, SWITZERLAND, 2003. THE CANAL RETAINED AS A PUBLIC SPACE AND THE LIBERATED . MODEL.

[GEORGES DESCOMBES]

The 1991 project for the *Voie Suisse* (Swiss Way) commemorated 700 years of the Swiss Confederation. Rather than creating a series of distinct monuments, it was decided that a more fitting memorial would be to create a commemorative route that circled Lake Brunnen. How do you tell such a complex historical story to the visitors? Is it possible to relate political history through the vehicle of the landscape? We decided that our project would not be a memorial to sorrow but instead to the cleverness of the Swiss and their fantastically democratic ways. Memories are found in the archives as well as in the landscape, and there we supported our study of the territory. We looked at pictures of rich foreigners who vacationed in Switzerland and Swiss farmers poor and barefoot. We looked at the terrain and the old roads that circled the lake. We looked at the flowers and plants that grew on the hillsides. These would be the materials for the Swiss Way. Then we created a credo by which we would work: We would never add anything which had not been there before; instead we would intensify these elements and their effects. To upgrade an existing belvedere, for example, we surrounded it with layers of chain-link fencing [6–6]. When you have one million people coming to the site you have to ensure their security. This was specified in the client's brief. But you also have your

[6–6]
GEORGES DESCOMBES,
VOIE SUISSE, LAKE URI,
SWITZERLAND, 1991.
THE BELVEDERE.
[GEORGES DESCOMBES]

own brief. So at times I play the role of the real client—the people. In fact, I may be our best client.

Memory can come from the situation, position, alteration, but also from associations with materials. We uncovered the remains of a road from the Napoleonic era. Where it needed physical reinforcing, we rebuilt low walls. Where the path needed definition we added an edging of concrete blocks. In places the contours were too steep to allow walkers to change direction comfortably, so we stepped the land in a way that recalls the famous grass staircase by Alvar Aalto at the town hall at Säynätsalo in Finland.

In Switzerland we have a lot of cows and a lot of boulders. And boulders, as we know, are very nearly memorials in themselves. Erratic boulders have traveled long distances on glaciers. Some are white, and their white surfaces reflect the sunlight, allowing them to travel far beyond the point as which darker rocks would have been deposited. Carmen Perrin, an artist with whom we collaborated, cleaned several of these boulders of moss and dirt with the help of art students from Geneva [6–7]. Cleaning intensified their visual presence as well as revealing their beauty—and their history. Washing uncovered memory. Nothing more was needed.

[6–7]

CARMEN PERRIN,
VOIE SUISSE, LAKE URI,
SWITZERLAND, 1991.
SCRUBBED BOULDER.
[GEORGES DESCOMBES]

A MEMORIAL AND TWO PARKS

In 1992 an El Al cargo plane crashed into a housing district on the edge of Amsterdam. Some months after the unfortunate event we were asked to make something there in response, to make a memorial to those who had died as a result of the crash. The people who lived there said: "We want something for our sorrow." I thought the form of the memorial should be low, even flat; I didn't want to give it any vertical dimension so that it would be quieter. We based the plan on the footprint of the buildings that had been destroyed, and at the very spot of the crash there would be a fountain [6–8]. But away from the exact point of collision, the memorial would be park-like; there would also be a landscape connection to the city. In the end the memorial is a kind of a dialog between sorrow and life. When you carefully consider the nature of the site, when you design a project for a particular spot, there are no true limits. The physical limits of the project are not the conceptual limits of the work, neither in time nor in geography. The idea of the project encompasses a space far larger than the actual limits of the intervention.

　　Our entry to the competition for the redesign of the Lustgarten, the park in front of Karl Friedrich Schinkel's Altes Museum in Berlin, was intended as a quiet statement. During World War II, the Nazis used this space for political

[6–8]
GEORGES DESCOMBES,
BIJLMEMEER MEMORIAL,
AMSTERDAM, THE
NETHERLANDS, 1998.
THE MEMORIAL SEEN
FROM ABOVE SHOWING
THE TRACE OF THE
BUILDING FOOTPRINTS
AND FOUNTAIN.
[GEORGES DESCOMBES]

rallies as a manifestation of their force. And after the war, the Communist regime used the "floor" of this space in just the same way. We felt an appropriate solution would be to plant the Lustgarten in such a way that the trees in the park would not block views of the Altes Museum colonnade [6–9]. To accomplish this, we proposed digging down, lowering the level of the floor in such a way that the crowns of the trees would just reach the original ground level. In this sense, the park was treated as an anti-monument. As we want no more tanks, at any time, we planned to dig into this paving, into this "floor of horrors" with its collective history of mistreatment. In the process we would discover the white sand that is the foundation of Berlin. So instead of accepting the paving from the Nazi years, we would use the sand—white sand—as a setting to display selected archaeological pieces from the surrounding museums. It would have been a very quiet garden with trees and sun that afforded the possibility for looking out from the Altes Museum over a carpet of green leaves.

The Parc de la Cour du Maroc, which opened in 2007, provides much-needed green space to the communities living in the neighborhoods near the Gare de l'Est in Paris. Deriving from land occupied in the past by railroad lines, the shape of the site was long and linear: 100 meters by 500 meters [6–10]. And rather than fighting the thrust of the site's geometry,

[6–9]
GEORGES DESCOMBES,
LUSTGARTEN PROJECT,
BERLIN, GERMANY,
1994.
[GEORGES DESCOMBES]

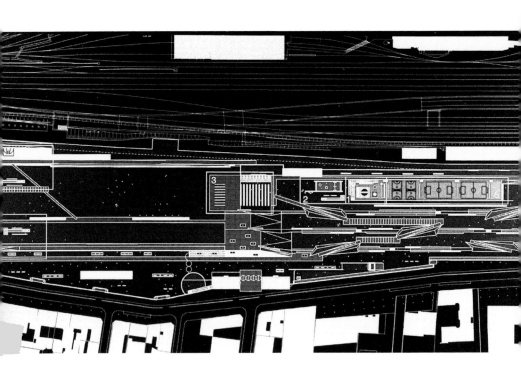

[6–10]

GEORGES DESCOMBES
AND ADR,
MICHEL AND CLAIRE
CORAJOUD,
AND CARMEN PERRIN,
PARC DE LA COUR DU
MAROC, PARIS, 2007.
SITE PLAN.
[ADR]

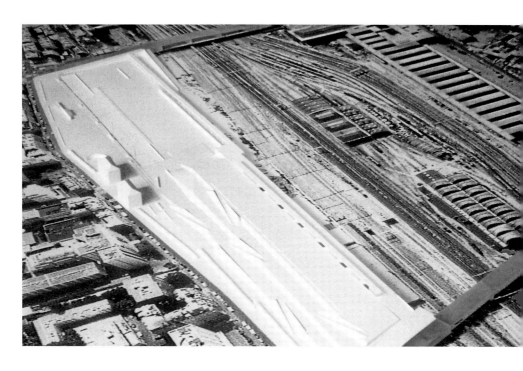

[6-11]
PARC DE LA COUR DU
MAROC, PARIS, 2007.
COLLAGE WITH
MODEL AND SITE
PHOTOGRAPH.
[ADR]

rather than chopping the land into several smaller pieces, we accepted the linear organization suggested by the proportions of the lot and its past as a locus of railroad infrastructure. We accepted, even exaggerated the confusion of buildings, infrastructure, and uses in and around the site. In reality, we won the competition because we addressed every demand made by the inhabitants and local activists. To use an analogy drawn from musical notation: we considered the linear geometry of the railroad tracks as our "staves;" the elements of the park would be the "notes;" together they would form the composition [6–11].

You see, for example, the echo of train tracks within the park in a long, planted gravel bed that in some ways serves as the armature for the park's design. Gravel also helps to disguise the real use of this part of the park. Nowadays it is difficult for any park department to accept the maintenance of sand boxes for play, so in response we named this particular feature the "gravel garden"—it certainly must be the longest sand box in Paris. We also wanted an ambiguous device at the back of the site to soften the edge between the park and the field of train tracks at the rear of the station. Ambiguity is also apparent in the perforated double-brick wall by Carmen Perrin. From some angles the voids prevail and the wall appears visually permeable. From other points, however, it reads as solid brick. Moving position changes your perception of the wall, as it does with many other elements of the park's design.

[6–12]
GEORGES DESCOMBES,
JEAN-LUC GODARD
STUDIO, GENEVA,
SWITZERLAND, 1978.
[GEORGES DESCOMBES]

A SMALL STUDIO

In closing, let me describe a small work I made with Jean-Luc Godard, the film-maker, to transform a former grocery shop into his small studio in Geneva. In some ways it too is a memorial; but it was a very nice project because it was so personal. At that time—some 20 or 30 years ago—we had neither email nor fax, so for written communication we had to exchange telegrams. But here in this project we had two aspects of memory. One was the remains of a kitchen—a sink and a water faucet. Godard wanted this to be kept just as it was. "Don't get rid of this," he said. "My father was a doctor. He was always washing his hands: leave that so I will think of my father when I wash my hands." The second aspect: in the process of transformation, we pulled down several partition walls and a part of the heating system. When we were finished with demolition a single column stood right in the middle of what was to become a TV studio [6–12]. Godard and I thought it was perfect as it was and that we should leave the column. But one of the video technicians became furious, saying to Godard: "You're crazy." He had never seen a TV studio with a heating system in its center. Godard said to him calmly: "You know, you have worked in Hollywood, in Berlin, in big studios with all the writers and the playwrights, but, I am a little arts-and-crafts kind of guy. I have to do everything myself. I have to do the writing—and to write I have to walk. So I don't want to remove this column because I need to have something to walk around. I need that column."

In our work one aspect of selective preservation has been that of memory and the past; the other has considered the present and the future. But perhaps, as Fuentes told us, we need to recall the future and imagine the past. Both address our memories in some way.

ADAPTED BY
MARC TREIB
FROM A LECTURE BY
GEORGES DESCOMBES
PRESENTED AT
THE SYMPOSIUM
"SPATIAL RECALL:
THE PLACE OF MEMORY
IN ARCHITECTURE
AND LANDSCAPE,"
HELD AT THE
UNIVERSITY OF
CALIFORNIA, BERKELEY,
ON 10 MARCH 2007.

[7]
Land,
Cows,
and Pyramids

Adriaan Geuze

All the projects designed by West 8 address the issue of memory in some way: for some projects it lies hidden behind the surface and is not an obvious concern; in other works memory is a central factor—either in terms of how we frame the project or in the sources that influence our thinking. It's important to emphasize that having been born in the Netherlands, I have lived with environmental and social conditions that differ radically from those of other countries [7–1]. To begin with, I was born three meters below sea level, a condition which has to have affected my perspective on the landscape and my ideas about how it should be created, designed, and managed.

THE NETHERLANDS

Much, if not most, of the Netherlands is a human creation, reclaimed from the sea over a period of centuries. Our history is one of constantly testing the laws of water: every canal in Holland is straight, and every one will stay like that. We are not afraid of the straight line that announces human intervention, and we don't give up dreaming that we can improve natural evolution. This attitude has brought about a special kind of society. At times we may have to laugh at this society, but nevertheless it continues to attempt to be something distinctly Dutch.

In some ways, even the very existence of the Dutch landscape remains a miracle—a reputation that can be overwhelming. There is no landscape in the world that is really close to our landscape, either in terrain, water management, or character. That's what I believe. It's a landscape born every morning from the clouds, from the fog, and in both summer and winter—perhaps half the year—there may be rain that attacks the land almost horizontally. Due to the flatness of drained land, even from eye level one can see great distances, a property that has been a central element in Dutch art over the centuries.

Today this landscape is heavily threatened by Dutch society itself. Due to the nature of our living and working patterns, commuting is taking its toll on the land. Rather than commuting from the periphery to the center of the city like many other metropoles, we commute from city to city. We have the pleasure of commuting to school, to work, or to

[7–1]
WEST 8, BORNEO-
SPORENBURG DISTRICT,
AMSTERDAM,
THE NETHERLANDS,
1993–1997.
[WEST 8]

our grandmothers in landscapes that until recently have looked like paintings by Rembrandt or Jacob van Ruysdael. That's our prevailing belief about the Dutch metropolis: the smaller city conglomerate within a beautiful Dutch landscape. However, in the 1970s the Dutch gave up planning and results have not been positive.

At that time we created an enormous bureaucracy for the planning of traffic and development, a bureaucracy which today involves more than 100,000 lawyers, urban planners, architects, and engineers. They have a lot of work—it's a machine to supply jobs. But this is all paper, and the reality is that without an effective and intelligent plan the Randstad—the area between Rotterdam and Amsterdam—is rapidly changing into a Los Angeles or Jersey. And with every change in government, every four to five years, there is a new National Planning Strategy. They praise the landscape and they praise the Randstad; they praise not being a metropolis like London. But in reality, Holland is becoming like Los Angeles. Nobody tells the truth, and that's what was irritating me and others of my generation. The area in the center of the Netherlands is referred to as the "Green Heart." That is to say, it has been green historically, but today any local mayor can plan for all kinds of resorts within a supposedly protected area of reclaimed land. The agricultural industry has been enormously successful by growing flowers and plants in glass houses, and this too has become a common image of the contemporary Dutch landscape.

But on the other side, government institutions founded to protect and celebrate the landscape advance plans that kick the farmers out, replacing authentic landscapes with clichés of leisure and recreation parks. This is the landscape produced by the current generation in positions of power. How does this landscape accord with our memories of the Dutch landscape passed down through time? Of course, this landscape has been decided by politicians who love the landscape so much that they give it the kiss of death. In time even the politicians begin to feel badly about the sprawl they have helped to create. And because they appreciate the landscape near where Rembrandt and Mondrian both painted, they help heal the landscape into a grotesque quasi-nature. As a result, with help from landscape architects, some of the most beautiful open landscapes became a forest park and lost their horizon. Even more devastating than these changes in landscape type is the sprawl that is today 100 percent American, especially in the southern part of the Netherlands. And due to national and European regulations about noise levels, a new freight train line running from Rotterdam to Germany suddenly brought 120 miles of concrete wall that blocks every north–south view. This plank, some 7- to 18-foot-high, has the same appearance as the former Berlin Wall and spoils the landscape. Nobody asked for it, but it is there.

What about childhood memories? When my father thought I should see cows when I was a child, it took about five minutes by bicycle to reach one; now it takes more than an hour to bike from the city center to the countryside. Something substantial has been lost, and in terms of Dutch heritage this is really sad. And if in winter you cannot ice skate from your house to the first cow within ten minutes, something is lost. I wonder what experiences my own children will recall when they have become adults.

While this may seem humorous to a foreign reader, I feel this attachment to non-urban land is the pure essence of Dutch culture. In the 1990s the younger generation protested heavily

against a new kind of planning document from The Hague that proclaimed the need for one million new houses. The need may have existed, but 90 percent of these houses were to be suburban. The call was, say, approximately 100,000 houses every year for ten years, almost all to be built over existing meadowland. To protest such a rash project, and to illustrate the scope of the project, we planned to construct a model with one million houses to be located on the Hague's Parliament Square. It would have taken us a full day to install, and therefore we weren't allowed to set up the model—as a Dutch citizen you are given only half an hour to make your statement. Of course, The Netherlands is a democracy but you cannot claim a part of the square for an entire day—there are some 20 other groups with similar statements they wish to make.

So instead of building the model in Parliament Square we asked the Netherlands Architecture Institute in Rotterdam to install the model within the museum. To illustrate the enormity of the number "one million" we proposed to use every space in the complex: the toilets, the library, every exhibition hall, the entrance, the lobby, the cafeteria—everywhere—because we needed the entire museum, every square meter, for the model. The institute, like our national democratic government, didn't like our concept either, so we built the model on the street beneath the institute's archives [7–2, 7–3]. Thirty students installed the pieces, and we spent an entire day completing

[7–2] *above*
WEST 8,
A SEA OF HOUSES,
NETHERLANDS
ARCHITECTURE
INSTITUTE,
ROTTERDAM, 1995.
[WEST 8]

[7–3] *opposite*
A SEA OF HOUSES,
NETHERLANDS
ARCHITECTURE
INSTITUTE,
ROTTERDAM.
[WEST 8]

the project. The model told us something else besides the scope of the number "one million." It also showed that there is no use in having any planning for the houses: if you build that many houses, it doesn't matter how they are laid out. This is one of the lessons we learned.

Cows have been on my mind for at least a decade. A more recent project, and one that resulted in serious media attention, was to address the Dutch landscape as we all know it. To provoke Dutch commuters we planned to occupy vacant areas along the highways we knew would be developed within ten years. We planned to install a set of giant billboards in the form of a cow, an enormous cow. But what sort of cow should be pictured? A lonely cow, a crying cow? We finally decided to take the most famous cow in Dutch history—the cow in Paulus Potter's seventeenth-century painting—translating the image into a giant billboard [7–4]. We put up three billboards on which these cows addressed commuters on the highway, telling them that a horizon is not a given, but is in actuality a very precious thing. They should celebrate and preserve the horizon, and deter any development that would destroy that wonderful view of cows over the land. In all, you might say that we were trying to maintain actuality as the stuff for future memories, as well as maintaining old memories in the present and future.

Four years ago we decided more serious and scientific research into the history of Dutch land reclamation. Our

subject was the nearly 50 percent of the country's territory which has been reclaimed since the tenth century. We now know exactly where they are, how big they are, when they were founded. We made a list with some 4,000 names, with dates, years, and categories—this is the Dutch landscape, man-made; this is the landscape taken from the sea. Most of the landscape was born between the eleventh and thirteenth centuries, created primarily by monks and farmers. Due to the manner of reclamation some land remained a perpetual swamp while other parts oxidized and sank. Finally, in the fourteenth and fifteenth centuries, the land was well beneath sea level and during those centuries a series of storms and high seas wiped out the land. The catastrophe of the St. Elisabeth flood in 1421 came to symbolize this era: it inundated most of the county and the area near Dordrecht disappeared. The reclaimed land was not just submerged—it was literally eaten by the sea. The sea swallowed the soil; it was gone. Thirteen villages disappeared, a traumatic disaster that stimulated the need for a new logic in Holland: the culture of the Dutch. They realized they needed dikes.

So they built dikes around every piece of land to protect the polders against the sea. And when you build dikes you need pumps to get the water out, so the windmill needed to be invented. By the sixteenth century the windmill technology had become so elaborate that an incredibly new culture emerged. Let's say that they literally took the sea, built a dike around it, and pumped the water out. They really claimed the seabed. That was a really stunning concept in the sixteenth and seventeenth centuries and as a result the landscape grew massively. Within 30 years the old delta-shaped area was reclaimed in the sixteenth century. The art of landmaking synchronized with the birth of the nation: the Republics independents from Spain. The success stemmed in part from a new type of windmill whose head could be rotated to face the wind; this made the windmill ten times more efficient.

And then another miracle began: pumping out the deep lakes north of Amsterdam. The Dutch were overwhelmed by this new landscape. They liked it so much—they were really hypnotized by this beautiful new landscape—that they started to see it as the subject for paintings. Like Don Quixote these painters magnified the presence of the windmills, dazzling horizons with hundreds of these miracle machines to feed their imaginations. This had never been done before; landscape painting, with the landscape alone as prime subject, was invented. Ruysdael, Vermeer, Hobbema, Van der Velde made the genre important. Rembrandt always saw the landscape as open: the flat land, the clouds hiding the sun, the beam of light on a farm. He composed portraits like such landscapes.

In the eighteenth century the Dutch slept; the English took over. But then in the early nineteenth century, incredible catastrophes struck Holland's river areas. In severely cold winters ice in the rivers congealed as enormous dams, and then the dikes broke everywhere. This phenomenon happened three times in 25 years and more than half of the Dutch landscape was unusable. For 30 years they gave up the idea that they could ever control the flooding, but finally the steam engine appeared. A new corps of engineers took control and they drained very deep lakes using steam-driven mills with a capacity far beyond even today's diesel-driven pumps.

At the same time as new lakes were being pumped dry a new colonization began in the peat district in the north, and there were new fantasies of reclaiming the entire inner lake, a large district called the Ijsselmeer. For 30 years they dreamed of reclamation, and then an engineer named Lely proposed a plan to build a dam that would split the lake from the sea and create four new polders. The plan was implemented by a clever mixture of research and engineering, again illustrating the Dutch spirit for creating home land and its mastery of the means by which to accomplish the plan.

These projects also involved some degree of social engineering: designing schools before the land was made, assigning farmland, organizing communities. They simply brought forward a coherent planning method that integrated science, culture, farming, society, engineering, and democracy. Everything became part of one great operation. And this operation resulted in polders larger than any others that had preceded them. The new landscape born since the 1920s was more splendid than even in Rembrandt's time. Photographers made their documents, which are photos reflecting the culture of the painters, of course. I consider these as beautiful Zen gardens.

World War II and the loss of Indonesia—as well as the Cold War and the disastrous flood of 1953—accelerated the pace of need for water control. A new technology arose and a new design and research industry developed. An early computer now controlled the entire waterworks on one side of the Netherlands. And with the new post-war technologies they built more dams, further canalized the rivers, and created more reservoirs of fresh water. There was a scale and splendor to these landscapes that is almost American. Then the baby-boom generation took over. They changed the national perspective from one focused on the physical landscape and land-making to one more centered on social and economic issues; they rebuilt systems for education, for national health care, for institutions. As in other countries these ambitions didn't result in a better society, but undermined the quality of health care education and resulted in inert bureaucracies. The concern for the social and economic agendas in isolation from the landscape ruined the country and to some degree the environment as well. We believe that we must rediscover our old tradition of creating land, with each generation proposing its own model world.

For a number of years West 8 has tried to create ideas and projects and alternatives that reflect this debate and that could positively provoke a direction. We researched an alternative for the extension of Amsterdam with a capacity of approximately 45,000 houses, renewing the ecological situation of the Wetlands, and upgrading the efficiency of the water system using the old understanding of the system as a whole, rather than one based on small parts taken individually.

A few years ago Al Gore came to the Netherlands, and two months later, even Bill Clinton arrived. Of course our prime minister greeted them warmly. Gore explained the threat of rising sea level to this man-made land on the sea bed. Although this was generally known, since then our prime minister talks about is as well. West 8, as a design office, launched a polemical project addressing coastal defense using a series of seaborne islands build as large landfills. To reinforce to validity of the project we collaborated with the dredging industry.

Twenty miles out from the Dutch coastline—starting in Calais, France, and extending as far as Den Helder, in the

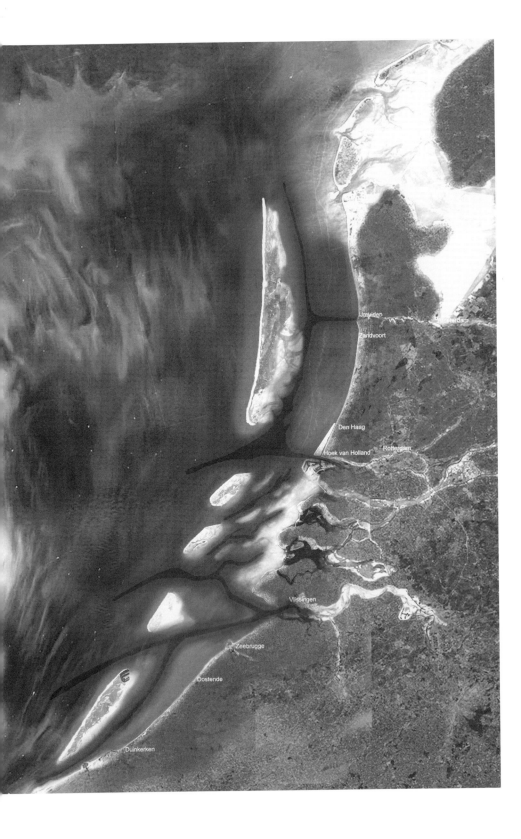

north of Holland—we would construct a new coastline, with artificial islands, like those in Dubai and Singapore [7–5]. The Dutch and Belgian dredging industries are world leaders in the field, but even for them such a project would take a generation. The reclaimed terrain would be immediately occupied as both these countries already need significant amounts of land. The dredging operations will also result in an undersea canyon to serve as sanctuary for sea life, a project certified by the World Wildlife Foundation. This was a paper project, addressed to the media. The Dutch seashore could be protected from heavy waves by adding completely new coastlines beyond the horizon, producing a new system of lagoons behind it. The shape of the Islands and the manipulation of the undercurrent also guaranteed a sea level drop during storms from the northwest. In this way we tried to review the impotence of the Dutch planning machine, to remind them that Holland itself is a sort of project of reinventing nature. The Dutch planning bureaucracy should be revitalized; it should stand in its own heritage of landmaking.

.

EGYPT

The Grand Egyptian Museum competition, which drew nearly 800 entries from an international field, was won in 2002 by the Ireland-based architects Henegan and Pang. The site, which is under UNESCO protection as a World Heritage site, enjoys a spectacular desert setting on the Giza Plateau near Cairo. The architectural concept cast the museum as an excavation into the plateau that also forms its new face; the geometry of the scheme derives from the various sight lines to the pyramids, which are illuminated at night.

The young architects who won the competition had to assemble a team for realizing the project. As a result, a team of consultants, including West 8, was asked to prepare the master planning for the landscape as well as more detailed designs for public spaces and some gardens. The scale of the proposed building is nothing short of colossal, with giant corridors that are the principal features of the museum architecture. This is actually a museum with no style, but rather a generic design whose beauty derives principally from its triangular grid and

[7–5]
WEST 8, OFFSHORE ISLANDS, NORTH SEA COASTLINE, 2007.
[WEST 8]

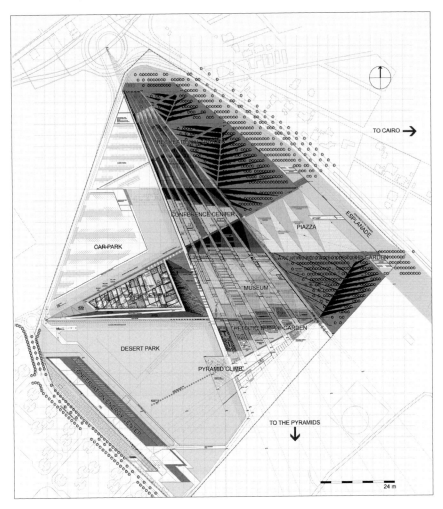

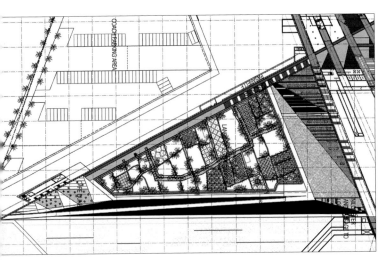

[7-6] *opposite above*
WEST 8,
LANDSCAPE ARCHITECTS;
HENEGAN AND PANG,
ARCHITECTS;
GRAND EGYPTIAN
MUSEUM, GIZA,
2004–2009.
MASTER PLAN.
[WEST 8]

[7-7] *opposite below*
GRAND EGYPTIAN
MUSEUM, GIZA.
GARDENS PLAN (DETAIL).
[WEST 8]

[7-8]
GRAND EGYPTIAN
MUSEUM, GIZA.
ENTRY COURYARD WITH
STATUE OF RAMESSES II.
[WEST 8]

its resulting view of the pyramid—and from its size: the façade, for example, extends about 2,500 feet and will be made of translucent alabaster. Along its edge the museum measures about 240 feet in height. It's really huge, and by some measures, grotesque.

The museum will be dedicated completely—100 percent—to the display of artifacts, virtually none of them intact. In Egypt 100,000 artifacts are discovered each year and for a long time UNESCO was really worried that these objects would not be preserved and scientifically categorized unless there is a museum large enough to contain this vast collection. When West 8 joined the design team we questioned the absence of the vital Nile landscape in the concept of the museum and its collection. If we bring the entire world to Egypt, to this museum, and to the pyramids at Giza—here we're talking about 10,000,000 visitors a year—we have the responsibility for explaining to them how ancient Egyptian society was based on the Nile, on something other than broken artifacts and rocks, dust, and desert. We argued to the client team that in the West the perception of Egypt is preoccupied with the clichés of desert, camels, and pyramids. We discussed with them that the museum and the exhibition lay-out should more accurately present ancient Egyptian civilization. Cairo doesn't look like the Nile River Valley, refreshed and fed periodically by flood. Instead visitors encounter a cityscape that looks dusty, stinking, rocky, and broken—really hot and unpleasant.

We argued that, within the museum context, we should represent in some way the old Egyptian landscape and geology—that the cultural and landscape phenomena need to be explained in relation to the Nile. With this basic idea, with this riverine memory, we tried to reinvent the original design in collaboration with the architects [7–6]. We proposed that the space fronting the museum needed to be green as a visual part of the Nile Valley. The client team adopted this idea, and really pushed the concept that the land of Egypt—the Nile system, the gardens, the herbs—should be integrated in the entire museum as a single entity.

The second problem we were facing was that Cairo, which now has 12,000,000 people living within its metropolitan area, has started to extend to Giza. The city has grown rapidly in recent decades, swallowing or polluting an enormous amount of land that once had the potential to be green. Development was displacing the desert. For this reason UNESCO declared Giza a World Heritage site. Our master plan is also part of the UNESCO designation.

A boulevard runs the full length of the plateau edge, linking the Sphinx and the museum. A shuttle uses the boulevard to bring visitors from the cheap parking areas set further away. Even before the museum has opened every major hotel chain has tried to buy land at Giza and if nothing changes the skyline will be made by American hotels rather than pyramids. The master plan needed to address these pressures. The third important intervention, which we are finalizing at the moment, is the design of the integrated design of the Land of Egypt. A triangular piece of desert land at the back of the museum will be excavated some 70 feet below the level of the desert to form a sunken green court with a layout representing the flood plain of the Nile.

Considerable research into the water system and its drainage preceded the design of this area. With archeologists, we will rebuild some historic pumps to show visitors how the water system worked; some fields will be inundated; we will grow crops and plants from the old days. There have already been considerable scientific studies about what the pharaonic herbs were, what kind of food the ancient Egyptians had, and so forth. At the ends of the museum, there will be a series of linear gardens, where we will reconstruct temple gardens and those used to grow herbs used for mummification [7–7, 7–8]. Drawing on the efforts of the scientists we are able to reconstruct and present these plants to visitors. The boulevards leading to the museum and the parks around it will also provide people from Cairo, who have no parks in which to meet one another in shaded greenery. The triangular motif will prevail in the design.

A selection of archeological fragments from Luxor will be displayed outside the museum before they are eventually rebuilt and moved into the museum. And last but not least, behind its alabaster facade the museum will have an enormous atrium. Because of its gigantic dimensions we felt that the

atrium needed some element to provide a sense of scale, depth, and three-dimensionality. We thought to use one of the original pharaonic statues for that purpose. We proposed moving the statue of Ramses II—many of these still exist in Egypt, but few are intact—into the courtyard from the square in front of the Cairo train station [7–9]. Surprisingly, the Minister of Culture supported the idea, and then, believe it or not, about two years ago—and covered by CNN—3,000,000 people in Cairo and the entire world watched Ramses make his journey to the site. (The project, executed by Italian archeologists and specialists, was sponsored by Western corporations, of course). Now it's standing on the site, protected from the sun. All of this, now under construction, will constitute a scientific research institute where all the artifacts—100,000 artifacts each year—will be brought and categorized, and then safely brought into the museum through a tunnel.

While the designs of Grand Egyptian Museum developed, we became extremely excited about this project and the way in which landscape architecture contribute to the efforts of preserving and explaining ancient Egypt. We are neither a scientists nor an archeologists, but simply by looking at the living Egyptian landscape, seeing the frescoes and artifacts, and reading the literature our own memories and stereotypes have been restructured. By emphasizing the importance of the landscape to the project, we felt we have added a little to the scientific mission as well as the tourist experience. In fact, adding the consideration of the memory of landscape did change the entire project.

[7–9]

WEST 8,
LANDSCAPE ARCHITECTS;
HENEGAN AND PANG,
ARCHITECTS;
GRAND EGYPTIAN
MUSEUM, GIZA,
2004–2009.
PALM-COVERED
GARDENS.
[WEST 8]

ADAPTED BY
MARC TREIB
FROM A LECTURE
BY ADRIAAN GEUZE
PRESENTED AT
THE SYMPOSIUM
"SPATIAL RECALL:
THE PLACE OF
MEMORY IN
ARCHITECTURE AND
LANDSCAPE,"
HELD AT THE
UNIVERSITY OF
CALIFORNIA, BERKELEY,
ON 10 MARCH 2007.

[8]
The Mediterranean Cemetery: Landscape as Collective Memory

Luigi Latini

Related to interment, the use of the word "landscape" in southern Europe is still imprecise, despite the ambiguous and disconcerting fascination that "landscape" presently enjoys there. Nor do cemeteries exist in any single form. "Graveyard islands" have become places of isolation and loss of boundary, overwhelmed by urban sprawl and profound changes in the countryside. In other places the original notion of the *camposanto* (churchyard or holy ground) still sporadically survives, holding out against the pressures of major social change. In addition, contemporary architecture offers us models and symbolic messages often far removed from the meaning of death held today by modern society. Clearly, there is today neither agreement nor any single approach to the design of landscapes for the dead. Even so, the collective memory of burial roots it in a landscape as a funerary ground. This perception, which is intrinsic to the southern European tradition, largely disappeared in the second half of the twentieth century, but has resurfaced in certain enlightened—though dissimilar—examples and locations. These examples provide some hope for a renewed cemetery culture.

Over the last decades only a few isolated projects of great merit have been produced in this field which has almost always followed architectural trends. These landscapes represent a small minority of work in a situation where burial grounds have distanced themselves from contemporary social life: part of those "disappearing" processes which Jean-Didier Urbain described at length.[1]

If a modern Italian "way of death" has ever existed in architecture, modern journalism has only accentuated a figurative awareness of the issue. Writing has excessively focused on certain selected works—Aldo Rossi's Modena Cemetery, for example—but has concealed a general absence of ideas and projects and, above all, the role that landscape can play in the contemporary perception of death. Consideration of the "Mediterranean" landscape in this field belongs to more spirited cultures, like the resurgent Catalan culture, rather than the more conservative Italian ethos. The potentials of landscape, together with their significant connections to a changing society, have been explored more conclusively in a

[8-1]

ENRIC MIRALLES AND CARMEN PINÓS, IGUALADA CEMETERY, SPAIN, 1990. FAMILY BURIAL VAULTS.
[LUIGI LATINI]

climate of socio-cultural renewal, such as that which Barcelona experienced during the 1980s. The Igualada Cemetery by Miralles and Pinós, and the Rocques Blanques project, both to be discussed later, are examples of this attitude [8–1].[2]

The common Italian attitude towards cemetery design remains conventional, and the natural/informal order of the so-called English-style burial ground continues to clash with the abstract/formal order of a cemetery constructed of geometrically configured stone, marble, and gloomy evergreens. In the first instance, landscape expresses a desire to find consolation for mortality, an obvious return to the order of nature. In the second case, the structured shape of the graveyard represents a society waiting—or rather, according to Christian belief "sleeping"—where natural shapes accompany the geometry of a symbolic figure, of a formalized nature. The landscape, off stage, expresses the earthly dimension of this anticipation, the theater of human experience. A broad view of southern European landscape traditions would suggest that when entering a cemetery in this part of the world a person finds him- or herself halfway between two approaches. These are the geometrical, transcendental order of the garden (the *camposanto*, the sacred ground) and the pastoral order of the surrounding landscape (the image of human experience left behind).

Cemeteries in the English style, built by the numerous Anglo-Saxon communities that have migrated south, can be read as designs adrift within the suburban outlines of Mediterranean coastal cities. This has been true since their first informal conception and importation to the Mediterranean countries by expatriates. They demonstrate how impossible it is to recreate an aesthetic model tied to a feeling of nature in a southern climate. One such landscape is *il buio giardino straniero* (the dark foreign garden) described by Pier Paolo Pasolini upon entering the English Cemetery in Rome, a modern Rome no longer linked to its original elegiac vision of ruins.[3] Here Pasolini searches for a different meaning of holiness and the mystery found in other landscapes, set within an ancient world touched by modernity.

In the construction of southern European cities it is normal to think of the "landscape" as based on models and clichés that have prevailed over the last two centuries, formal models—from romantic gardens to functionalism—arising from a philosophy of, and sentiment toward, nature belonging to different cultures. The feeling of a lost link between places and collective memory can possibly be found by contemplating this process of assimilation. As already mentioned, the cemetery in southern Europe is an artificial place, like a garden, conceived in a broader landscape matrix that gives it identity. In contrast, in the north the cemetery comprises an entire landscape, artificially constructed in the picturesque–romantic tradition, to express the meaning of burial.[4]

THE MODERN ATTITUDE

The modern attitude toward landscape that emerged in the twentieth century introduced a different sense of distance to the idea of burial. It significantly modified the perceived relationships between buildings and place reflected in the direction of the paths which crosses them. The Woodland Cemetery outside Stockholm (Gunnar Asplund and Sigurd Lewerentz, 1915–1940) concentrates many of these aspects in a single example [8–2]. The sense of place is based on the sacred significance of a pine forest, rejecting the cliché of a "funereal landscape park" in the sense of a scene reproduced from antiquity, painting, or history. Its landscape is cast as a meditation on the value of distance, infused from its conception with suggestions of a "journey to Italy" which perhaps ironically helps to evoke a deeper perception of the northern forest. Above all, its "processional" dimension evades any temporal or stylistic definitions. The buildings, in constant relationship with each other along the path and in its resting places, show the commemorative role of a tangible landscape as in the Italian *sacri monti* (sacred mountains).[5]

Contrary to common opinion, during the "modern" years —even in Italy—landscape was considered to be the guardian of meaning linked to memory and commemoration. There are examples, however, in which landscape no longer plays merely a complementary role in relation to the building, or a role as only decorative scenery. Instead it expresses the emotional and evocative importance of the place. The idea of the sacred no longer relies on the symbolic language of monuments. It is no coincidence that in the 1960s certain figures linked to Italy's industrial development stimulated a renewed consideration of burial grounds with designed landscapes that expressed personal and collective memory while shunning the rhetoric of traditional monuments.

[8–2]

GUNNAR ASPLUND AND SIGURD LEWERENTZ, WOODLAND CEMETERY, ENSKEDE, SWEDEN, 1915–1940.

CHAPELS SEEN BEYOND THE MEDITATION KNOLL. [MARC TREIB]

In this return to origins, the burial ground represented a secular/religious feeling for the landscape. In the middle of the Venetian countryside where she was born, Rina Brion looks at the enclosure for her tomb designed by Carlo Scarpa. This cross between the tomb and the garden was visualized by the architect as a path between buildings wedded to their site [8–3].[6] Entry through the existing cemetery insured a connection between the old and the new, between the Brions and the community. In addition, the tomb's formal plan announces its extending of the Italian cemetery tradition.

There are other significant examples of this way of thinking, but it is better to first review the several stages that have shaped funereal culture in southern Europe and its controversial relationship with the landscape. The projects of the architect Ferdinando Fuga, for example, perfectly express the spirit of eighteenth-century reform, of a modern vision which gave rise to the great exodus of the dead from the ancient city. Surely the most startling expression of this mentality was the cemetery of the 366 trenches in Naples.[7]

In 1762, directed by the King of Naples to solve the problem of overcrowding in urban graveyards, the so-called

Camposanto Nuovo (New Cemetery) and the 366 trenches were conceived as a terrible funereal machine set on a hill facing the Gulf of Naples. A simple square fence surrounds 366 holes dug into a bare ground surface. These openings give access to underground chambers where each day the anonymous bodies of the city's destitute population were thrown. Every day a different trench was opened in numerical order. The openings are distributed in rows of 19, in boustrophedon order —that is, numbered alternately from left to right and from right to left. In this way the daily chore of opening the graves proceeded in a linear fashion with the same practical mechanism used by oxen when ploughing fields.

Here, the cemetery is a tabula rasa, an empty space. The Neapolitan burial ground is a *non lieu* lost in the essence of time; with a cold, rational spirit it anticipates that wish to challenge the places and funereal rites belonging to late-eighteenth-century Paris, places and funereal rites that repeatedly re-emerge, even in the functionalist approaches of the 1970s.[8]

Antonio Niccolini, like Fuga, was a Tuscan serving in the Neapolitan court.[9] In several drawings of the Pisan Camposanto, Niccolini anticipated, with the vision of a stage designer, the secular idea and symbolic significance that graveyards were to acquire in the following centuries. Here the enclosed area is no longer a place without ties to the world beyond it. Instead, it now possesses an inside and outside: urban society finally recognizes itself and its own destiny in the architectural structure which it occupies—the four-sided portico and central impluvium and the magnificent scenery of the mountains in the distance [8–4].

The famous Pisan burial ground was conceived as a sort of architectural "relic" and it was immediately called a *campo-*

santo because Pisan ships brought "holy" earth here from Palestine during the Crusades. Tradition holds that this earth consumed the buried bodies within a few days, to the amazement of many "grand tourists" from Britain and other countries.[10] Above all, works of art in the Camposanto assume a symbolic quality of time, conjured by the many archaeological funereal artifacts brought here, among them those removed from the sacristy of the cathedral nearby. This sort of anti-quarium is an early example of the secular idea of a cemetery in which man recognizes the value of individual burial as well as a sense of history and the civilization to which he belongs. The composite image of the cemetery conceived as a promenade and a museum triumphs over the identity of individual monuments. It is a world revealed by the reciprocal relationship of things encountered along the way. This was a planning strategy common to the picturesque tradition, although now expressed in different ways, with the Père-Lachaise Cemetery in Paris as the prime example.[11]

The symbolic position and evocative force of the so-called "graves of the valorous" disappeared with the nineteenth-century middle class, giving way to the emotive, completely extroverted, and melodramatic scenes of Staglieno in Genoa and Montjuïc in Barcelona. The realistic description of familiar scenes, of individual prosperity, established the rules for a new landscape, although the typological origin of the grave-yard was little different from the Pisan holy ground [8–5].

The cemetery became a unanimous and tangible vision of society, ordered in its internal structure on the basis of a shared social hierarchy. It was no longer a meditative and philosophical promenade but instead the representation of a living world. In its configuration, however, the burial ground

belonged to a place—to its topography, climate, and scenery which themselves are expressions of a shared memory: the Tyrrhenian coastline, the horizon of the Lombard plain, or the lagoon; the outlines of a mountain or a lake; or even the pattern of a suburban landscape melting into the country-side. The cemetery occupied a place where everyone could recognize his or her own experience of life [8–6].[12]

Many of these ties with the locale were lost during the process of urbanization in the second half of the twentieth century, and the habit of exalting social position and individual and family fortunes became a detrimental factor. This was a trend particularly noticeable from the 1970s onwards, when overcrowded cemeteries oscillated between pitiless functionalist places under public management and an ancient tenure over private and individual relationships with burial.

LANDSCAPE AS COLLECTIVE MEMORY?

While the 1930s produced collective monuments steeped only in rhetoric—particularly the cemeteries of the Great War—from the 1960s on, architectural culture produced some interesting reverberations. These accompanied industrial shifts and the movement of peasant society into the big cities. Some people questioned the fate of the Italian landscape precisely in those years in which a process of transformation had begun on a scale without precedent. In spite of the lack of interest in the theme of cemeteries, Italy was surprisingly well documented in the second edition of *Modern Gardens and the Landscape* by Elizabeth Kassler. Her book included two cemeteries discussed later in this chapter: Pirago-Longarone by Gianni Avon, Marco Zanuso, and Francesco Tentori, and San Vito di Altivole by Carlo Scarpa.[13]

During these years, discussions in Italy centered on the results of two competitions which ended the historic chapter of nineteenth-century cemeteries although without any conceptual evolution. The first competition, held in Urbino in 1973, proposed a form which provided its own references: a furrow in the soil as the evocation of an ancient ritual—the catacombs of early Christianity—but with a link neither to the population nor to the surrounding landscape. It was one of the first appearances of an artist—in this case, Arnaldo

[8–5]
STAGLIENO CEMETERY WITH THE BISAGNO VALLEY LANDSCAPE BEYOND, GENOVA, ITALY.
[*CAMPOSANTO DI GENOVA*, c.1910]

Pomodoro—in the field of landscape architecture.[14] The second competition, in Modena in 1971, proposed a city suspended in time alongside the enclosure of the neoclassical cemetery. This project was justifiably popular with critics and photographers but instantly aroused consternation among the citizens of the city.[15]

In post-war Italy, Pietro Porcinai and Maria Teresa Parpagliolo Shephard were the leaders of a minority of practitioners who explored the international boundaries of a new branch of learning: landscape architecture. With their peculiarity of being designed for one purpose, war cemeteries gave landscape architects an opportunity to experiment with new ideas. Maria Teresa Parpagliolo designed the French military cemetery at Monte Mario in Rome in 1944 at the top of a hill, with explicit reminders of a secular idea of the "Italic landscape." Her design deliberately referenced the debate concerning the protection of Italian landscape which was in its first fragile stages of development.[16] The path of memory leads through sunny terraces where the graves are set beneath olive trees, long evergreen hedges, and avenues framed by holm oaks, cypresses, and great *Pinus pinea* that enlarge the scale of the setting for the collective spaces [8–7].

The exploration of the Italian landscape as an expression of collective memory, somewhat ironically, has usually been linked to international figures rather than Italians. Among

[8–6]

CAMPIGLIA MARITTIMA, LIVORNO, ITALY.
THE PARISH CHURCHYARD WITH THE TIRRENO SEA COAST IN THE BACKGROUND.
[LUIGI LATINI]

the many German military cemeteries on the peninsula, the work of two Germans—Walter Rossow, landscape architect, and Dieter Oesterlen, architect—at the Futa Pass in 1969, merits citation [8–8A, 8–8B]. The site lies in the heart of the Tuscan-Emilian Apennines, an area of important sandstone quarries whose development and expansion were fuelled by the great efforts to construct cemeteries after the war. Collaborating with the German designers, Ernst Cramer, from Switzerland, contributed to the link between graveyard and local stone, suggesting the use of the same Italian workers he had used for his *Garten des Poeten*, created ten years previously in Zurich.[17]

The structure of the cemetery echoes the shape of the mountain, punctuated by terraces fanning out over the countryside, supported below by a massive stone wall in the form of an ascending spiral that runs from the entrance to the chapel at the top of the hill. The wall follows a path which links the 75 burial camps over two kilometers, creating space for 30,000 graves. While the road rises gently, the rows of stones run horizontally and continuously, without any break at their bends. Several stone reliefs emerge from the layers of this peaceful mass, including a stone seat alluding to rest and a cross rising from the sloping wall surface. The cadence of the crosses is reminiscent of the rhythm of a slow walk, as in a Via Crucis, all directed towards the opposite side of the

[8–7]
MARIA TERESA
PARPAGLIOLO
SHEPHARD,
MONTE MARIO
FRENCH MILITARY
CEMETERY, ROME,
ITALY, 1946.
[LUIGI LATINI]

[8–8A]
DIETER OESTERLEN,
ARCHITECT;
WALTER ROSSOW,
LANDSCAPE ARCHITECT;
GERMAN MILITARY
CEMETERY,
PASSO DELLA FUTA,
ITALY, 1967.
THE MAIN WALK
THROUGH THE BURIAL
GROUNDS.
[LUIGI LATINI]

[8–8B]
GERMAN MILITARY
CEMETERY,
PASSO DELLA FUTA,
ITALY.
POOLS.
[LUIGI LATINI]

slope, where the eye is drawn towards the solemn scenery of the surrounding mountains. This suspended, dignified dimension of walking produces a sense of measure to the path, keeping its distance from the overwhelming dimensions of the gigantic common grave.

More tragedies, more mountains. In the years following the collapse of the Vajont Dam in October 1963, the Pirago cemetery was built nearby. Here too, the designers Gianni Avon, Marco Zanuso, and Francesco Tentori questioned the presence of the mountain and how the landscape could suggest new forms of commemoration.[18] The area of the little burial ground, a plateau surrounded by high mountains, looks like an elongated field interrupted by a furrow in its center. A single track around the graves and burial vaults crosses this fissure, widening and narrowing in several places as needed. A stone wall encircles the cemetery without interrupting the view beyond. The visitor enters and descends the path that runs through the trench, immersed in a situation somewhere between the familiar proximity of the graves and the presence of the mountains beyond the boundary walls.

In the same area as Vajont, in the new Erto a Monte Cemetery (designed in the same years by Glauco Gresleri and Silvano Varnier) four simple terraces combined the rite of visiting the deceased with a perception of the wider world. All that remains of this place are the photographs taken soon after the inauguration; the community immediately rejected this experience, which they did not at all understand.

The idea of a terraced burial ground possibly belongs to sunny southern cultures, and the idea persists to our day. The Roques Blanques cemetery, designed by Enric Battle and Joan Roig, was built in 1985 on the fringes of the densely

packed Barcelona suburbs [8–9].[19] Its design managed to
construct spaces and landscapes that reveal a society largely
composed of immigrants from the poor regions of Spain. The
graveyard is situated on a steep slope between two valleys in
the Sierra de Collserola. The land is mostly wooded, with
pasture land and arable fields located at its southern end.

The plan and architecture of the cemetery are adapted
to the land, recalling the shapes and images of both the local
agricultural landscape and the Mediterranean garden. Groups
of terraces follow a single road that retraces an existing agricultural track. The burial ground uses the vocabulary of the
garden on the terraces covered in packed earth: pergolas covered with vigorous wisteria or jasmine shade the graves along
the walls; sparse plantings of trees—palms, pines, Judas trees,
plane trees—are distributed informally; the outside edge of
the terrace consists of a continuous bench, facing the surrounding woods. The terraces, on leaving the main road,
become a private place for meditation and meeting among
the living—just as in a garden.

Pietro Porcinai, a Florentine landscape architect, and
Carlo Scarpa, a Venetian architect, were unusual in twentieth-

century Italy for being among the very few to have designed gardens with an innovative spirit. They were also involved in the design of cemeteries, a form of meditation on the *dolce piano*, as Dante called the vast plain which covers the north of Italy. At Bascapé, in the plain between Pavia and Milan, Pietro Porcinai evoked with simplicity the significance of the death of three people in a tragic plane crash. Enrico Mattei, an important figure in the Italian industrial scene, was traveling with the pilot and a journalist in 1963 when their flight ended tragically.[20]

A stream and a dirt road run over the land disrupted by the impact of the airplane, curving to follow the orthogonal mosaic of the cultivated fields. The water, the geometry of the rows of poplars, and the horizon of the plain were the triggers for this project which used the landscape as a living expression of a consciousness linked to memory [8–10A]. The stream was diverted into a canal that surrounds the whole field. Inside the great tree-lined enclosure a pattern of right-angled paths outlines a second enclosure delimited by rocks. Here, three oak trees record the burial of the three men. Today, 40 years later, the field has reached maturity in the developing life of the garden. The pattern of the cobbled paving on the grassy plain and the accompanying shrubs now contrast with the vertical thrust of the great bald cypresses. Porcinai chose these trees to form a sober screen around this secular camposanto, surrounded by water and immersed in the Lombard plain [8–10B].

In the cemetery of San Vito di Altivole in the Asolo foothills, the grave of the Brions occupies a great enclosure set between parish graveyard and cultivated fields. Its buildings and open spaces possess a constant reciprocal relationship

that surrounds the tomb of the married couple: a covered path; a spacious lawn and the enclosure; a chapel surrounded by water; a pool containing a pavilion. This funereal landscape, designed by Carlo Scarpa between 1970 and 1978, can be interpreted as a garden. Even Carlo Scarpa used the word "garden" to explain the project in his lecture in Vienna in 1976. To Scarpa the word "garden" suggested "to the Venetian society, small, tranquil society—different ways to approach death which can be social and civil."[21] The relationship between the site and the personal story of the Brion family is the key to the project. The site, treated by Scarpa as a narrative, represents the memory of the unfolding of a common experience: in the vision of the Brions this enclosure acquired the significance of a sacred site. The landscape can be glimpsed over the top of the wall and through its fissures; with the church and the outline of the hills with the Asolo Fortress in the distance: "for this reason," said Scarpa, "I call the boundary wall sacred land, because from within one has a magnificent view…"

The tomb and setting for the Brions, in many ways idyllic, could justifiably close my discussion, but I must

[8–10A]
PIETRO PORCINAI, MATTEI MEMORIAL, BASCAPÉ, PAVIA, ITALY, 1963. CONSTRUCTION PHOTOGRAPHS. [PIETRO PORCINAI ARCHIVE, FIESOLE]

return to the sense of tragedy more typical of Mediterranean sentiment. I will end by mentioning some *fossar*, places of execution and common burial, whose memory is still alive in Spanish society. Much has been said about these sites and how the landscape can express the memory of a still vivid wound.

The Fossar de la Pedrera, hidden on one of the slopes of the Montjuïc hill in Barcelona, is a place of silent pilgrimage for Catalans [8–11A, 8–11B]. Here, on the fringes of the city's great urban cemetery, a quarry was used during the years of Spain's Civil War as place of mass execution and common burial. Through the years, the bottom of the quarry has been filled with unauthorised crosses and muddled signs of recognition. The project, promoted at the beginning of the new era of democracy in Catalan society, aimed at expressing the meaning of a visit to a place of collective memory within a single episode: the grave of the Catalan President Lluís Companys who was shot there.

The architectural structures, finished in 1986, are simple narrative reminders that reinforce the dramatic quality of a place in which prevail the emotive strength of the high rock

[8–10B]

MATTEI MEMORIAL, BASCAPÉ, PAVIA, ITALY. SWAMP CYPRESSES SURROUNDING THE MAIN FIELD. [LUIGI LATINI]

faces that frame the sky above.[22] A ramp winds upward toward the quarry entrance; its paving invites a slow, pensive pace. A dark colonnade of cypresses and stone pilasters, engraved with the names of the victims of the 1939 executions, marks the narrow access to the quarry and prepares the visitor for the next stage. Beyond, the bare walls of the quarry present a sober image, in contrast to the simplicity of the great lawn bordered on one side by the curved line of a long bench. In a single sign, the lawn and bench concentrate the tragic significance of a burial ground that has lost every trace of individuality.

Ayanadamar, just outside Granada, is the name both of a spring and of a place of a *carmen* which in the Arabian Middle Ages offered the most fabulous gardens, luxuriant cultivations, and pleasure grounds. In the center of the garden, the spring water gushes and gurgles into a pool made in the shape of an eye: *Fuente de las lagrimas* (*Ayanadamar* in Arabic) is the name given to this spot.[23] Near the spring is a memorial

[8–11A]
BETH GALÍ,
FOSSAR DE LA
PEDRERA,
MONTJUÏC,
BARCELONA, SPAIN,
1986.
ENTRANCE
APPROACHING
THE CYPRESS
GROVE.
[LUIGI LATINI]

to the poet Federico Garcia Lorca who was shot and buried in a common grave together with all the other victims. An olive tree near this source marks the probable location of his grave.

The possibility of unearthing the poet's remains is being discussed today. The political parties, once opposed, now strongly wish to disinter his remains—but the poet's family insists and prays that the serenity of the site should not be disturbed. Memory is becoming a question of pure ideology. Why create a new project when the landscape already expresses its history, the history of a culture tied to the life of a single man?

At this moment, Mediterranean culture does not require more monuments. Instead, it needs to develop a new, respectful, and imaginative relationship with its own landscape. To understand the place occupied by the dead in this landscape provides both the designer and the culture with a suitable point of departure.

[8–11B]

FOSSAR DE LA PEDRERA, MONTJUÏC, BARCELONA, SPAIN. THE FORMER BURIAL GROUND AT THE CENTER OF THE QUARRY. [LUIGI LATINI]

NOTES

1 Jean-Didier Urbain, *L'archipel des morts. Le sentiment de la mort et les dérives de la mémoire dans les cimetières d'Occident*, Paris: Plon, 1989.

2 Anatxu Zabalbeascoa, *Parque cementerio de Igualada Cemetery: Enric Miralles and Carme Pinós*, London: Phaidon, 1997.

3 Pier Paolo Pasolini, *Le ceneri di Gramsci*, Milan: Garzanti, 1957.

4 For an overview of landscape and cemeteries in southern Europe, see Luigi Latini, *Cimiteri e giardini: Città e paesaggi funerari d'Occidente*, Florence: Alinea, 1994.

5 On the *sacri monti* cited, the particular Tuscan example of San Vivaldo, and Battisti's studies on the subject, see "La topografia simbolica della Terrasanta nella prima fase cronologica dei Sacri Monti in Italia Settentrionale e centrale (1480–1525)," in Eugenio Battisti, *Iconologia ed ecologia del giardino e del paesaggio*, Florence: Olschki, 2004, pp. 291–307. On the Woodland Cemetery, see Caroline Constant, *The Woodland Cemetery: Toward a Spiritual Landscape. Erik Gunnar Asplund and Sigurd Lewerentz 1915–61*, Stockholm: Byggförlaget, 1994.

6 Luigi Latini, "Cimiteri e disegno del giardino nel paesaggio italiano del Novecento," in *All'ombra de' cipressi e dentro l'urne. I cimiteri urbani Europa a duecento anni dall'editto di Saint Cloud*, Bologna: Bonomia University Press, 2007, pp. 202–205; Luigi Latini, "Porcinai a San Vito di Altivole. Il contributo del paesaggista fiorentino," in *Memoriæ Causa. Carlo Scarpa e il complesso monumentale Brion 1969–1978*, Treviso: Fondazione Benetton, 2006, pp. 24–25.

7 Francesco Lucarelli, *La vita e la morte. Dal Real Albergo dei Poveri al Cimitero delle 366 Fosse*, Lecce: Edizioni del Grifo, 1999.

8 On eighteenth-century burial reform, and a discussion of new cemeteries beyond the city walls, see Grazia Tomasi, *Per salvare i viventi. Le origini settecentesche del cimitero extraurbano*, Bologna: Il Mulino, 2001.

9 Anna Giannetti and Rossana Muzii, eds, *Antonio Niccolini, Architetto e scenografo alla Corte di Napoli (1807–1850)*, Naples: Electa, 1997.

10 Clara Baracchini and Enrico Castelnuovo, eds, *Il Camposanto di Pisa*, Turin: Einaudi, 1996.

11 Richard Etlin, *The Architecture of Death: The Transformation of the Cemetery in Eighteenth-century Paris*, Cambridge, Mass.: MIT Press, 1983.

12 On the historical Italian cemetery, see Maria Giuffrè, Fabio Mangone, Sergio Pace, and Ornella Selvafolta, eds, *L'architettura della memoria in Italia. Cimiteri, monumenti e città 1750–1939*, Milan: Skira, 2007; for a bibliography on the same theme, see Luigi Latini, "Luoghi della memoria. Disegno e cultura del paesaggio nei cimiteri e nei memoriali italiani," in Luigi Zangheri and Lucia Tongiorgi Tomasi, eds, *Bibliografia del giardino e del paesaggio italiano 1980–2005*, Florence: Olschki, 2007, pp. 95–103.

13 Elizabeth B. Kassler, *Modern Gardens and the Landscape*, New York: Museum of Modern Art, revised edition 1984.

14 On the extention of the Urbino Cemetery, see Francesco Leonetti, ed., *Il cimitero sepolto: Un progetto di Arnaldo Pomodoro per Urbino*, Milan: Feltrinelli, 1982; and Giulio Carlo Argan, "La collina sfagliata: il cimitero di Arnaldo Pomodoro per Urbino," *Lotus International 38*, 1983, pp. 56–58.

15 On Aldo Rossi's San Cataldo project and other entries to the "concorso nazionale di idee" for the cemetery's enlargement, see the special issue of *Controspazio*, October 1972.

16 On the work by the Italian landscape architect Maria Teresa Parpagliolo Shephard (1903–1974) and her Monte Mario project, see Sonja Dümpelmann, *Maria Teresa Parpagliolo Shephard (1903–1974). Ein Betrag zur Entwicklung der Gartenkultur in Italien im 20. Jahrhundert*, Weimar: VDG, 2004, pp. 208–219.

17 On the cemetery at the Futa Pass, see Udo Weilacher, *Visionary Gardens: Modern Landscapes by Ernst Cramer*, Basel, Birkäuser, 2001, pp. 126–131.

18 On the Pirago Cemetery near Longarone, Belluno, see Renato Pedio, "Cimitero di Longarone, Belluno, architetti Gianni Avon, Francesco Tentori, Marco Zanuso," *L'architettura cronache e storia*, 232, 1975, pp. 632–637; and Laura Bertolaccini, "Cimitero-memoriale di Longarone, Avon, Tentori, Zanuso," *Area*, 63, 2002, pp. 98–111.

19 "Cimitero metropolitano Roques Blanques," in Ignasi de Solà Morales, *Architettura minimale a Barcellona: Costruire sulla città costruita*, Quaderni di Lotus 5, Milan: Electa, 1986; and "Terrasses dans la vallée, *Pages Paysages 3*, 1990/91, pp. 170–177.

20 On the project for the Mattei memorial by Pietro Porcinai (1910–1986), see Luigi Latini, "Cimiteri e disegno del giardino nel paesaggio italiano del Novecento," in *All'ombra de' cipressi e dentro l'urne*, pp. 202–205.

21 Of the many publications on the Brion tomb, I would just mention the recent works by Vitale Zanchettini, *Carlo Scarpa. Il complesso monumentale Brion*, Regione del Veneto; Venice: Marsilio, 2005; and Erilde Terenzoni, ed., *Carlo Scarpa: I disegni per la Tomba Brion*. Inventario, Milan: Electa, 2006. The text of Scarpa's lecture "Può l'architettura essere poesia?" given on 16 November 1976 at the Academy of Fine Arts in Vienna was published (in part) in Carlo Scarpa. *Opera completa*, Milan: Electa, 1984; and thereafter in *Casabella*, 562, 1989. This talk includes his comments on the Brion project.

22 "El Fossar de la Pedrera," in *Barcelona espais i escultures (1982–1986)*, Barcelona: Ajuntament de Barcelona and Fundació Joan Miró, 1987, pp. 124–127.

23 José Tito Rojo and Manuel Casares-Porcel, *El Carmen de la Victoria. Un jardín regionalista en el contexto de la historia de los cármenes de Granada*, Granada: Editorial Universidad de Granada, 1999.

Esther da Costa Meyer

Memory preys on places: there are virtually no un-situated recollections. Yet the mind exacts a price for preserving the past. Recollections are the fruit of conflict and compromise, indelible but unstable. Taking nineteenth-century Paris as my example, a city undergoing violent urban and political change as a result of both industrialization and the revolutions of 1830, 1832, 1848, the coup of 1851, the Franco-Prussian War, and the Commune, I wish to explore the intersection of memory and the built environment that followed these dramatic changes of regime and the attendant iconoclastic consequences. Though Paris witnessed the destruction of huge swaths of urban fabric throughout the century, during the Second Empire (1850–1870) piecemeal interventions gave way to a concerted effort to overhaul the French capital, led by Napoleon III and his prefect, Georges-Eugène Haussmann. By then, the old historic center, the Île de la Cité, and adjacent parts of the Right Bank, had become a vast slum, with tottering tenement buildings and dark, narrow streets [9–1]. The area had been devastated by the cholera pandemic of 1832 which coincided with yet another popular revolution, and the government and the leisured classes came to associate the impoverished quarters with both disease and insurgency. Prompted by political as well as hygienic concerns, the government razed the winding alleyways and rotting houses which barely allowed sunlight to trickle down to street level. Though Haussmann also tore down mansions and palaces belonging to the aristocracy, the bulk of the destruction was aimed at the derelict housing stock that served as home to the poor and to segments of the middle class, either in the center or in strategic districts required for the broad new boulevards that would henceforth criss-cross the city.

Parisians complained bitterly of having lost their bearings in what they perceived as a dystopic metropolis. "Blessed are the provincials, the real provincials! They do not move house. Their home belongs to them ... It overflows with traditions and memories," lamented a contemporary:

> But we martyrs of the Parisian civilization, camping like nomads under our tent, like Bedouins in the desert, we scatter our lives throughout this vast Sahara of stone, in twenty banal dwellings none of which will preserve our traces.

[9–1]
CHARLES MARVILLE,
*RUE DU HAUT-MOULIN
(SEEN FROM THE RUE
GLATIGNY)*,
PARIS,1865–1866.
[BIBLIOTHÈQUE
ADMINISTRATIVE DE
LA VILLE DE PARIS /
ROGER-VIOLLET]

> The tracks of our feet efface themselves behind us as if
> they were written on sand.[1]

It is hardly surprising that the destruction of cherished homes and familiar streets and squares was experienced as a traumatic ordeal: architecture plays a crucial role in self-definition, giving—or denying—stable points of reference, havens which citizens can call their own and where they feel protected [9–2]. Any site can offer support for associations and subject formation.

Baudelaire's friend, the writer Alfred Delvau, echoed this feeling of dispossession but he focused on the destruction of historical landmarks at the height of Haussmann's campaign of urban renewal:

> This evisceration of what was once Romanesque, then
> Gothic, then Renaissance Paris, then the Paris of Louis XIV
> —this evisceration is something profoundly melancholic
> for the artist and for the dreamer who find themselves
> disoriented as they contemplate the past and interpret the
> dramas of our history... for those who can see and hear,
> [stones] can speak—and do so with eloquence [9–3].[2]

For Delvau the burden of memory is displaced to architecture which relays highly selected views of the past to successive generations, telling them who they are and where they are coming from. Monuments of historic or aesthetic importance do not always trigger the same deeply felt emotional response

[9–2]
DEMOLITIONS ON
THE RIGHT BANK
DURING THE OPENING
OF RUE DES ÉCOLES,
PARIS.
[L'ILLUSTRATION,
26 JUNE 1878;
BIBLIOTHÈQUE
NATIONALE DE
FRANCE]

as modest homes and neighborhoods. Yet they too help shape identity, collectively in this case, rather than personally. They amplify the individual. "Architecture is to be regarded by us with the most serious thought," wrote Ruskin. "We may live without her, and worship without her, but we cannot remember without her. How cold is all history, how lifeless all imagery, compared to that which the living nation writes, and the uncorrupted marble bears!"[3]

Conversely, the idea that the new architecture erected by the regime had no memories was widespread. The strident new buildings of the Second Empire were often felt to be amnesic, untenanted by souvenirs. In the words of the writer Jules Claretie:

> Between the quai d'Orsay, on the left, and the quai de Billy, on the right, the Seine flows between superb buildings, but [buildings] without memories, arrogant and new, buildings that do not evoke a single image nor speak of a specific past.[4]

It is memory, whether that of a single person or a social group, that invests a particular location with singularity and significance, and thus separates place from the undifferentiated sameness of space.[5]

Haussmann's aggressive form of redevelopment did not target architecture and urbanism alone, but landscape and topography as well. To make room for new streets and squares, many gardens were razed, along with several hills that obstructed traffic. Entire parts of the center, including all its bridges, were leveled or lowered to facilitate circulation. In 1867, as the capital was being embellished to host the World's Fair, the authorities shaved 15 meters from the top of the colline de Chaillot, where the Musée d'Art Moderne now stands, to make the hill's profile less ungainly. Part of the resentment that greeted Haussmann's slash-and-burn approach to urbanism had to do with the fact that he also demolished sites—not just buildings—of historic importance, such as the Butte des Moulins between the Louvre and the Opera, the mound from where Joan of Arc had launched an unsuccessful assault against the British invaders in 1429 [9–4].[6]

Yet despite all vicissitudes, cities stubbornly resist total erasure. According to anthropologist Marc Augé, place is never completely effaced.[7] Buildings, streets, and even hills may vanish at a ruler's whim, but places have a resilience all of their own since meaning does not coincide with their physical limits but encompasses the trains of association which they evoke. The Bastille, a hated symbol of feudalism destroyed by the populace in 1789, continues to this day to serve as a

[9–4]
CHARLES MARVILLE, *DEMOLITION OF THE BUTTE DES MOULINS DURING THE OPENING OF THE AVENUE DE L'OPÉRA*, PARIS, c. 1877.
[MUSÉE CARNAVALET, PARIS/ROGER-VIOLLET]

rallying point for the Left. Another famous example of class-bound remembrance with regard to place was the old rue Transnonain in the center of the Right Bank where several workers had been massacred by the police in 1834, an event immediately memorialized by Honoré Daumier [9–5]. For two decades, the site endured as a powerful memento of class warfare until Haussmann finally destroyed the entire street. As he noted candidly in his memoirs: "It was the disembowelment of Old Paris, of the district of uprisings and barricades, by means of a wide central thoroughfare that pierced this almost intractable labyrinth."[8] Nevertheless, Daumier's lithograph kept the tragedy alive, and rue Transnonain joined the city's many "repressed topographies" which continue to resonate long after they are gone, sustained by publications, reproductions, and anniversaries.[9] In the heyday of the Second Empire, when thousands of inhabitants were displaced and their homes destroyed, Paris became a phantasmatic city, peopled by ghostly buildings and streets that were still part of the citizens' emotional and intellectual make-up. The affect generated by traumatic political events reinforced collective memory and enabled destroyed buildings and places to endure in human consciousness.

Places have many other ways of survival. The "persistence of the plan," underscored years ago by Marcel Poëte, and later by Aldo Rossi, reveals how modern cities are still determined by the "direction and meaning of their oldest artifacts."[10] In Paris the old Roman decumanus survives under a modern boulevard.[11] "Ancient Paris can be seen distinctly beneath the current Paris," wrote Victor Hugo in 1867, "like the old text between the lines of the new."[12] The unexpected intrusion of the past in the urban fabric was a common occurrence in Haussmann's day when the soil was constantly being dug up by his engineers [9–6].[13] Despite Baudelaire's memorable equation of modernity with the "ephemeral, the fugitive, and the contingent," the new Paris was in fact inseparable from the obstinate undertow of what came before. This metonymic relation of different pasts and presents afforded by old environments makes a mockery of historians' periodizations. As Aldo Rossi wrote perceptively:

> One must remember that the difference between past and future, from the point of view of the theory of knowledge, in large measure reflects the fact that the past is partly being experienced now, and this may be the meaning to give permanences: they are a past we are still experiencing.[14]

More modest records of urban history can be found in the gaps and openings of the urban plan. Some record ancient cattle trails, tow paths, or shortcuts taken by tradesmen—

water vendors or washerwomen seeking the river—the unheroic but meaningful annals of micro-history. Many still survive in the slant of a street or the widening of an artery where a stream once flowed and no construction was possible. In built environments, as Françoise Choay points out, there are no voids as such: "All non-built areas are nonetheless signifying elements."[15]

Toponyms constitute another great reservoir of urban memory. Cities, like Adam, are in the business of giving out names, beginning of course with their own. They endow sites, streets, and squares with specific meanings which have either accrued collectively over the years, or are attributed by fiat. In Paris, street names still recall the trades that once flourished in certain areas of the city like the rue de la Vannerie (basketry), rue des Fourreurs (furriers), or rue des Teinturiers (dyers). Other streets, rue de la Cerisaie (the cherry orchard) or rue Beautreillis (beautiful trellis), evoke the groves and gardens planted under the Valois kings. Many streets survive only in history books and Baedekers, like the rue de Jérusalem in the Île de la Cité, which once designated the starting point of the road that led from Paris to the Holy Land during the Crusades. The Marais, the elegant district where the aristocracy established itself in the seventeenth century, still recalls the *marais* (marsh), long since drained, that once covered the area. To Shakespeare's old question, "What's in a name?" cities respond with a litany of streets, buildings, and squares whose referents have gone missing and which constitute the fragmentary archives of remembered pasts.

The fight to preserve the memory of places by means of toponyms goes hand in hand with the formidable forces enlisted to destroy it. New rulers often change the names of streets and squares in order to memorialize their own dynasty. Throughout the centuries, different regimes have tried to politicize Paris's urban fabric by constantly re-naming its main arteries. With the secularization spearheaded by the French Revolution, Saint-Denis, for example, became Denis *tout court*, and Saint-Honoré was abbreviated to Honoré. Many other streets were given extravagant appellations. The First Empire put an end to these Jacobin procedures, replacing the names chosen by the revolutionaries with those of the military.[16] Under the July Monarchy, political dates were first used to designate streets, a tradition followed by the Second Empire. This assault on memory was but a new form of the *damnatio memoriae* of the ancients, the practice of political amnesia to eradicate all records of the person or dynasty overthrown by the new forces in power. In *The Book of Laughter and Forgetting*, Milan Kundera writes plaintively of "cities with nameless streets or streets with names different from the ones they had yesterday, because a name means continuity with the past and people without a past are people without a name."[17] This has been true of all cultures: place remains intact while associations change. Precious links to history are slowly severed from consciousness unless they reverberate powerfully in the collectivity.

Urban environments have other, more abstract ways of recalling places past, such as typologies or memory forms.[18] The type is what survives when the overlay of styles is stripped away to reveal the basic form, dimensions, patterns of fenestration, and general massing of particular kinds of buildings. Types codify the know-how handed down though generations in terms of customs, social and economic history, building trades, or climate. They persist stubbornly when all else changes, withstand war and insurgency, economic recession and fashion, and the successive avatars visited upon all cities, and constitute a form of urban memory that transmits knowledge about the interaction of architecture and society in specific places. To control unregulated construction along the new arteries, Haussmann imposed ordinances that limited the height of buildings and the number of storeys, and prescribed strict rules for entablatures, cantilevers, cornices, balconies, and publicity.[19] He redefined the type, in other words, and in so doing, preserved and transmitted it to future generations [9–7]. However, memories embedded in architecture do not faithfully reflect society's past but constitute a highly selective digest in which social classes and groups are not all represented equally. Types and archetypes, like many other traces of history embedded in architectural memory, tend to be normative, and represent what survives of the Darwinian social struggle recorded by architecture in its codes and buildings. Those structures that defy the passage of time are those constructed with stronger materials. The hovels of the poor, cobbled together with friable, makeshift scraps, leave no lasting vestiges.

[9–7]
CHARLES MARVILLE,
RUE TURBIGO, PARIS,
c. 1877.
[MUSÉE CARNAVALET,
PARIS / ROGER-VIOLLET]

"Memories" of place are not exclusively anthropocentric, refracted through the human psyche. From the perspective of what French historians of the Annales School have called the *longue durée*, the earth, too, "remembers," and provides yet another medium for spatial recollection. Every year, in February and early March, when the snow melted and the waters rose, the Seine overflowed its banks, and sought its old prehistoric bed in the Right Bank. In 1863, as Charles Garnier was beginning work on the new opera house, the river flooded its foundations, situated in the fossil arm of the Seine. This was the source of the persistent legend of the subterranean lake beneath the opera, memorialized in Gaston Leroux's *Phantom of the Opera*.[20] The Second Empire's engineers accordingly lowered and narrowed the bed of the river, so that it no longer runs in its natural bed: within urban limits, the Seine is now a canal, an "artifact," as Matt Kondolf put it so vividly.[21]

Underground Paris is riddled with vestiges left behind by the antediluvial animals that once roamed the area, long before the river came into existence. The Seine is all that survives of a vast inland sea that covered the surroundings during the Tertiary, millions of years ago. By turns tropical or arctic, the climate nurtured different forms of prehistoric fauna and flora whose traces can still be found in the abandoned quarries of Montmartre. In the early nineteenth century, paleontologists, stratigraphers, and botanists like Georges

[9–8]

OPOSSUM FOSSIL FOUND AT MONTMARTRE, PARIS.

[GEORGES CUVIER, *ANNALES DU MUSÉUM D'HISTOIRE NATURELLE*, 1804.

JOHN BLAZEJEWSKI / PRINCETON UNIVERSITY]

Cuvier, Alexandre Brogniart, and Adolphe Watelet studied the fossil remains of plants and animals preserved in the seams of gypsum, and reconstructed the history of the site before the appearance of the human species during the Pleistocene [9–8].[22] By mid-century, Haussmann's engineers themselves were finding bones of prehistoric animals—an elephant just outside the city walls and gigantic turtles underneath a roadway—as they laid the foundations of the city's new infrastructure of water supply and sewage disposal far below the ground. Ironically, these discoveries that documented the shape and relief of Paris before Paris found their way into guidebooks and were far more present in the public's mind in the nineteenth century than they are today.[23]

The demolition of huge swaths of urban tissue locked loss and memory in a powerful vise, as nineteenth-century Parisians scrambled about to compile an archive of what was gone by all available means. "Each day," noted the writer Alexandre Privat d'Anglemont:

> the municipal or private pickax whittles away a chunk of old Paris. We must make haste to sketch its biography, lest these ruins from another age disappear entirely both from the memory of mankind and from the face of the earth.[24]

A decade earlier, faced with the destructions of the July Monarchy, Balzac had already prophesied that old Paris would survive exclusively in the work of the *flâneurs*, "those historians who have but one reader, for they publish a single copy of their work."[25]

And yet consigning the past to memory carries its own inherent problems. Modernity has questioned the very nature of remembering, and in so doing affected our untroubled and unselfconscious relation to the past. Freud's discovery of the unconscious has challenged the easy relationship between memory and its referents, by showing how inconsistent and deeply interested memory really is. If place cannot be completely erased, nor can it be unproblematically "reproduced," for the mind is not a warehouse where bygone facts and sites slumber passively and intact, but a creative laboratory where the past is tampered with and restored the way buildings are restored, with additions and deletions. Memory is interventionist:

[9–9]
RUE RAMBUTEAU
WITH LES HALLES
ON THE LEFT, PARIS,
c. 1900.
[ROGER-VIOLLET]

it magnifies, diminishes, adjusts, darkens, or illuminates places
that are no longer extant, transforming the past anew every
time it is called to mind, shorn of undesirable reminiscences,
embellished by wishful thinking, colored by present concerns.
Recollections that seem so deeply etched are partly of recent
vintage. From a psychoanalytical point of view, remembrance
of places past, like all forms of memory, is skewed by partisan-
ship, a collage of shards pieced together by a subject who no
longer has access to the complete site "as it really was."[26]

The mind misreads the past in numerable and often
ingenious ways. Space, even in memory, is a function of time,
and cities are above all a record of time. As they grow, para-
meters change, and with them perception. The rue Rambuteau,
cut through the most populous part of Paris in 1838 during
the July Monarchy, and seen in its day as a broad and majestic
thoroughfare, was dismissed in 1867 as an "imperceptible
alley" by the photographer Nadar [9–9].[27] Much the same
kind of discrepancy occurs in the mind, where buildings and
places have no intrinsic size. Childhood streets and homes,
which loom so large in memory, shrink to diminutive proportions when seen again from the perspective of adult life.
According to Freud, dreams of childhood may also be expressed

by a translation of time into space. The characters and scenes are seen as though they were at a great distance, at the end of a long road, or as though they were being looked at through the wrong end of a pair of opera-glasses.[28]

These distortions carry their own truths. The spaces of memory are wonderfully elastic: like cinema, which they seem to have anticipated, they can dilate and take in vast panoramas, or compress the focus to a close-up, a beloved room or a window, when time itself seems to slow down and stand still.

Memory is profoundly imagistic. Places evoked after they have vanished are usually pruned of other sense-based associations. The buildings we recall appear strangely silent as they never were in actuality and, having lost their materiality, remain remote and impalpable like stills in a film. Touch, sound, and olfaction, considered more primitive and less developed, are largely filtered out of our reading of the past, whether we are reconstructing fragments of buildings, civilizations or our own experiences of years ago. Yet haptic and audible cues, and even taste, can also serve as powerful engines that raise memories from oblivion.[29] Volatile and invisible, odor too has a strong connection to human emotions and can color the places we bring back to mind.[30] "The places we have known," wrote Proust, "do not belong solely to the world of space in which we situate them for our greater convenience. They were only a slim slice among contiguous impressions which formed our life at that time; the memory of a certain image is but regret for a certain moment; and houses, roads, avenues are as fleeting, alas, as the years."[31] Our memories have been heavily edited, not only by fear and desire, habit and prejudice, but by the hegemony of sight, the most abstract of our senses. That modernity has privileged sight as an intellectual tool is by now a truism that has spawned a culture industry.[32] Vision far outruns the other senses in its ability to memorialize place. Haussmann himself practiced a form of urban renewal aimed at reconfiguring the city in terms of urban tableaux: the long boulevards with terminating vistas were meant to be consumed visually, and were remembered as such, very differently from the close-grained fabric of old Paris, with its viscous propinquity, its sounds, and its smells.

Memory practices, subject to historicity, also change over time, and have a bearing on how one remembers. In the case of the ancient *ars memoriae*, elaborate techniques like the famous sixteenth-century memory palaces of Matteo Ricci which were used for oratory, memory was indeed a parasite that made use of specific buildings to memorialize contents that were extraneous to the architecture evoked by the mind.[33] Place was simply a storage unit for a hypertrophic memory. The relation between signified and signifier was arbitrary, and the Jesuits could well have lodged the same

points of discourse they wanted to remember in other mental promenades and imaginary spaces. The modern world has long since rejected these highly artificial mnemonic mechanisms in favor of more efficient tools of reproducibility.

In the nineteenth century, the emergence of new reproduction technologies led to a rising flood of texts and images that also served as a surrogate or support for memory. With the expansion of print culture to a mass audience, and the introduction of steel-cut engravings and later photography, the press had a mechanism that not only recorded buildings but also the very moment of destruction. Photography witnessed painful events, taking sides as it did so. After the Commune, when parts of Paris were still smoking from the fires, photographers close to the new government produced numerous albums of buildings destroyed by the insurgents, clearly skewed from an ideological point of view [9–10]. There was no sign of the bloodbath visited upon the men, women, and children brutally massacred by the troops of Versailles. Official memory wanted to preserve images of the ruins before they were painstakingly restored, as an act of accusation against the "Reds." Photographs play a powerful role as mediation, either relaying pertinent information or short-circuiting our own recollections which are gradually replaced by the prosthetic images provided by the camera. In the case of the Commune, they served not so much to sustain memory as to replace it after the fact.

Class itself played a preponderant role in shaping recollections. Nineteenth-century Parisians did not have identical memories: even when different social groups recalled the same buildings or parts of the city, reminiscences differed sharply. Years ago, the sociologist Maurice Halbwachs insisted, in opposition to Freud, that memory does not occur in a vacuum, but is influenced by social context.[34] As the destruction of the Colonne Vendôme in 1871 exemplified, the two extremes of the population interpreted sites of political importance in ways that were fundamentally opposed to one another: for some, the iconoclasm constituted a glowing feat of the working class, for the middle and upper classes, an unconscionable act of vandalism.[35] Wherever social classes are polarized, there are no classless memories.

Neither the historical sediments embedded in the built environment nor those insubstantial ones enshrined in memory remain intact. Time works on all of them, with its unfathomable alchemy, eroding and transforming the meaning and appearance of the originary core. Shorn of its fugacity, weighed down by additions and embellishments, the past hardens into representations. We cannot escape the politics of memory.

[9–10]
RUINS OF THE HÔTEL DE VILLE, DESTROYED DURING THE COMMUNE, PARIS, 1871.
[BIBLIOTHÈQUE HISTORIQUE DE LA VILLE DE PARIS / ROGER-VIOLLET]

NOTES

1 Bernadille (Victor Fournel), *Esquisses et croquis parisiens*, Paris: E. Plon et Cie., 1876, p. 309.

2 Alfred Delvau, "Coup d'oeil rétrospectif sur Paris," *Paris qui s'en va et Paris qui vient*, Paris: A. Cadart, 1860, p. 4.

3 John Ruskin, *The Seven Lamps of Architecture*, 1848, reprint, New York: Dover, 1989, p. 178.

4 Jules Claretie, "Les Places publiques, les Quais et les Squares de Paris," *Paris-Guide*, vol. 2, Paris: A. Lacroix, Verboeken et Cie., 1867, p. 1381.

5 Barry Curtis, "That Place Where: Some Thoughts on Memory and the City," in *The Unknown City: Contesting Architecture and Social Space*, eds, Iain Borden, Joe Kerr, Jane Rendell, with Alicia Pivaro, Cambridge, Mass.: MIT Press, 2001, p. 55.

6 In Paris, as in many cities stretching back to antiquity, it is difficult to extricate geology from history. Like one or two other hills in central Paris, the Butte des Moulins was not "natural" but resulted from human intervention. Pierre Pinon, "Paris en relief," in Bertrand Lemoine and Marc Mimram, eds, *Paris d'ingénieurs*, Paris: Editions du Pavillon de l'Arsenal/ Picard, 1995, pp. 68–69.

7 Marc Augé, *Non-Places: Introduction to an Anthropology of Supermodernity*, trans. John Howe, London: Verso, 2000, p. 79.

8 Georges-Eugène Haussmann, *Mémoires du Baron Haussmann*, vol. 3: Grands Travaux de Paris, Paris: Victor-Havard, 1893, p. 54.

9 The term "repressed topographies" comes from James Corner, "The Agency of Mapping: Speculation, Critique and Invention," in Denis Cosgrove, ed., *Mappings*, London: Reaktion Books, 1999, p. 232.

10 Aldo Rossi, *The Architecture of the City*, trans. Diane Ghirardo and Joan Ockman, Cambridge, Mass.: MIT Press, 1988, p. 59.

11 Laurent Olivier, "The Past of the Present. Archaeological Memory and Time," *Archaeological Dialogues*, vol. 10, no. 2 (July 2004), p. 212. In Paris, the main *decumanus*, the east–west artery in Roman cities, was probably the rue Cujas. It was crossed at right angles by the *cardo*, the north–south axis, consituted by rue Saint-Jacques and rue Saint-Martin.

12 Victor Hugo, "Introduction," *Paris Guide*, vol. 1, p. x.

13 The so-called arènes de Lutèce, uncovered unexpectedly in the 1860s, were destroyed and then rebuilt in a clumsy and belated attempt at preservation. See Colin Jones, "Théodore Vacquer and the Archaeology of Modernity in Haussmann's Paris," in *Transactions of the RHS* [Royal Historical Society] 17 (2007), pp. 171–174.

14 Rossi, *The Architecture of the City*, pp. 57–59.

15 Françoise Choay, "Sémiologie et urbanisme," *L'Architecture d'aujourd'hui* 132 (June–July 1967), p. 8.

16 Lucien Dubech and Pierre d'Espezel, *Histoire de Paris*, vol. 2, Paris: Les Editions Pittoresques, 1931, p. 71.

17 Milan Kundera, *The Book of Laughter and Forgetting*, trans. Michael Henry Heim, New York: Alfred A. Knopf, 1980, p. 157.

18 Rossi, *The Architecture of the City*, pp. 35–47.

19 Bernard Landau and Annie Térade, "La Fabrication des rues de Paris," in Lemoine, Mimram, *Paris d'ingénieurs*, pp. 98–99.

20 Gaston Leroux, *Le Fantôme de l'Opéra*, 1910, reprint Paris: Le Livre de Poche, 1959.

21 See Matt Kondolf, "Rivers, Meanders, and Memory" in this volume.

22 Georges Cuvier and Alexandre Brogniart, *Description géologique des environs de Paris*, Paris: Edmond d'Ocagne, 1835; Adolphe Watelet, *Description des plantes fossiles du bassin de Paris*, Paris: J.-B. Baillière, 1866.

23 Émile de la Bédollière, *Le Nouveau Paris*, p. ii. Louis Simonin, "Les Carriers et les Carrières," in *Paris Guide*, vol. 2, p. 1591–1595.

24 Alexandre Privat d'Anglemont, *Paris anecdote*, Paris: Chez P. Jannet, 1854, p. 171.

25 Honoré de Balzac, "Ce qui disparaît de Paris," *Le diable à Paris*, Paris: Hetzel, 1846, vol. 2, p. 13.

26 This was the dream of positivist historians in the nineteenth century, most famously Leopold von Ranke who claimed to reconstruct history *wie es eigentlich gewesen ist.*

27 Nadar, "Paris souterrain," in *Paris Guide*, vol. 2, p. 1584.

28 Sigmund Freud, *The Interpretation of Dreams*, trans. and ed. James Strachey, New York: Avon Books, 1965, p. 443.

29 Proust, who immortalized the sense of taste, fell back on the old metaphor of memory-as-architecture to illuminate the sudden appearance of involuntary memory which can be aroused through senses other than sight: "But, when nothing subsists of an old past, after the death of people, after the destruction of things, alone, frailer but more enduring, more immaterial, more persistent, more faithful, smell and taste still remain for a long time, like souls, remembering, waiting, hoping, upon the ruins of all the rest, bearing without giving way, on their almost impalpable droplet, the immense edifice of memory." Marcel Proust, *Swann's Way*, trans. Lydia Davis, New York: Viking, 2003, p. 47.

30 Anna Barbara and Anthony Perliss, *Invisible Architecture: Experiencing Places through the Sense of Smell*, Milan: Skira, 2006, p. 14.

31 Proust, *Swann's Way*, p. 444.

32 Modern architecture, too, has relied heavily on the sense of sight, to the detriment of the experience of place, as Juhani Pallasmaa has eloquently pointed out. See Pallasmaa, *The Eyes of the Skin: Architecture and the Senses*, Chichester: John Wiley and Sons, 2005, and his chapter in this volume.

33 Natalie Zemon Davis and Randolph Starn, "Introduction," *Representations* 26 (Spring 1989), p. 3. The two authors were making a general statement, and did not refer to memory palaces.

34 It was Halbwachs who introduced the controversial notion of collective memory. Maurice Halbwachs, *On Collective Memory*, ed., trans., and intro. by Lewis A. Coser, Chicago: University of Chicago Press, 1992.

35 Matt K. Matsuda, "Monuments: Idols of the Emperor," in *The Memory of the Modern*, New York: Oxford University Press, 1996, pp. 19–39.

We frequently encounter ruins in the paintings of Caspar David Friedrich: fragments of a Gothic past; ciphers of an eternal religion at rest within an ephemeral body; architectural repositories of centuries and lives and belief [10–1].[1] Something forlorn haunts these remnants of prior eras standing adrift in a forest or isolated on a mountainside. The arches and columns of brick and stone serve as reminders, vehicles for thought, stimulants for meditations on the transitory aspects of life. Here, terminated, are the remains of buildings once intended to far outlast the short span of human existence. But they did not.

While the ruin may be the quintessential Romanic element, in neoclassical eras the ruin often represented the remains of a Golden Age—as they did in paintings by Claude Lorrain and Nicolas Poussin.[2] In Poussin's *Et in Arcadia Ego*, three shepherds and a robed woman examine a tomb inscribed with those words and attempt to unravel the mystery of their meaning.[3] Set within a classical landscape with only sparse vegetation, distant mountains, and a heroic sky, the tomb displays signs of physical deterioration and, by inference, the passage of time. The Romans built upon the vestiges of Greek civilization; centuries thereafter, the artists and architects of Renaissance Italy excavated, integrated, and reinterpreted the incomplete fragments of Roman civilization. Each age recovered the achievements of its predecessors and utilized them to create contemporary works, new in form and spirit.

When the British came to Italy on their Grand Tours they too mused upon past civilizations as apogees of beauty. In 1820 John Keats began his "Ode on a Grecian Urn:" "Thou still unravished bride of quietness, Thou foster child of silence and slow time."[4] The ruin slows time and grasps the past as a part of the present, as it inserts the present within the past. But true appreciation depended on education, as the poet and landscape theorist Richard Payne Knight told us:

> Ruined buildings with fragments of sculptured walls
> and broken columns, the mouldering remnants of
> obsolete taste and fall magnificence, afford pleasure
> to every learned beholder, imperceptible to the ignorant,
> and wholly independent of their real beauty.[5]

And then they returned to England and built gardens. And they put fragments in their gardens, and when there were no fragments they built them.[6] There were temples to

[10–1]

CASPAR DAVID
FRIEDRICH,
ABTEI IM EICHWALD
(EICHENWALD ABBEY),
1809–1810.
OIL ON CANVAS.
[AKG-IMAGES;
GALERIE DER ROMANTIK,
BERLIN]

gods and virtues; they were built complete, like the Temple of Ancient Virtue at Stowe. Or they were built as ruins, like the Temple of Modern Virtue at Stowe—a sardonic commentary on the state of English governance.[7] After the dissolution of the Catholic Church by Henry VIII, its churches were stripped and devastated, leaving a plethora of ruins to be rediscovered and perused by the Romantics. At Studley Royal in North Yorkshire, for example, the skeletal remains of Fountains Abbey became the centerpiece for contemplation and aesthetic musings amid a water garden formed by damming the River Skell.[8] At nearby Rievaulx Terrace, Thomas Duncombe joined two classical pavilions with a grassed promenade whose prin-

cipal dramatic feature was a downward view of the ruins of Rievaulx Abbey [10–2]. Having no suitable ruin upon his land at Painshill in Surrey, however, Charles Hamilton erected his own ruin—the Abbey—for the contemplation, and, one assumes delight, of his family and guests.

Perhaps the fetish for the ruin found its most elaborate expression at the Désert de Retz outside Paris, built in 1782 by François Nicolas Henri Racine de Monville.[9] There the principal retreat was built in the form of a colossal column—suitably in ruins of course—with its jagged top itself a symbol of a lifespan far beyond the year of its immediate creation [10–3]. Today, the column house reads as a folly and little

[10–2]

THOMAS DUNCOMBE, RIEVAULX TERRACE, NORTH YORKSHIRE, ENGLAND, 1754. THE RUINS OF RIEVAULX ABBEY AS SCENIC HIGHLIGHT. [MARC TREIB]

else. Could any new construction—especially one of such obvious fabrication—really evoke the emotions stimulated by true ruins in a historical landscape?

TWO CHURCHES

How shall we—that is, modern society—regard the ruin?[10] We, too, use it as an *aide memoire*—or to be more academically fashionable a *lieu de mémoire*. But we also use the idea of the ruin to retard the fading of memory or to grant a sense of history to new construction. At times these two uses stand at cross purposes; at other times they are in near concord.

[10-3]
FRANÇOIS RACINE DE MONVILLE, COLUMN HOUSE, DÉSERT DE RETZ, CHAMBOURCY, FRANCE, 1782.
[MARC TREIB]

Two important religious projects from the decade following World War II integrated ruins into their fabrics as a significant element of their designs.[11] They were built in key cities of the two principal antagonists: Coventry in Great Britain and Berlin in Germany. Both cities had been catastrophically bombed during the war: Coventry as an industrial center; Berlin as the center and symbol of the German Reich. As peace returned and reconstruction began, two of the cities' principal churches lay in ruins: St. Michael's Cathedral in Coventry and the Kaiser-Wilhelm Memorial Church in Berlin.

Egon Eiermann received the commission to rebuild the latter church as a result of an invited competition in 1955.[12] He chose to follow a modernist path, first proposing a Miesian scheme that positioned architectural elements such as the church and bell tower on a rectangular plinth.[13] The ruin of the church and its bell tower destroyed in the bombing held no interest for him. Why should it? he argued. It served no function; it could shelter no one; its forms evoked pathos rather than inspiration. No one wanted to remember the horrors of the war, both those instigated by the German polity and those suffered upon them. "People will be able to tolerate this stump [the remains of the old church] for only a few more years," he said; for succeeding generations, for those who had not suffered through the war, the ruin would hold no meaning. It would be better to eradicate immediately all that was bad in the old and instead look forward to the new. The new design represented hope and optimism and the future. The ruin had no part in this vision.

The citizens of Berlin had other opinions, however, and their fierce protest forced Eiermann to rethink his scheme and ultimately to retain the battered body of the old church.[14]

[10-4]
EGON EIERMANN,
KAISER-WILHELM-
GEDÄCHTNIS-KIRCHE,
BERLIN, GERMANY,
1961.
[MARC TREIB]

[10–5]
BASIL SPENCE,
ST. MICHAEL'S
CATHEDRAL,
COVENTRY, ENGLAND,
1962.
[MARC TREIB]

Rather than integrating the old and the new, however, Eier-mann's strategy flanked the old with the bell tower and the new sanctuary [10–4].[15] He hoped, in vain as it happens, that in time vines would cover the ruins, diminishing their presence as a historical relic. In the end, quite to the contrary—in all probability due to the composite of old and new—the church has proved to be enormously popular for locals as well as the itinerant tourist population. That play between old and new construction creates a contretemps that yields a semantic complexity neither could have produced in isolation: the new informs the old, the old the new. We establish the present (and in some ways, also the future) by comparing it to the past. Should these rest in harmony or in resonance? Each appears as a viable direction.[16]

In contrast to the openness of the program for the Berlin church, the competition brief for the new St. Michael's Cathedral at Coventry required entrants to retain the ruins of the old church, although just how was not specified [10–5].[17] Even while the war still raged, art historians like Kenneth Clark had cast an effete and aesthetic eye on the destruction resulting from German bombardment, declaring that "Bomb

damage in itself is Picturesque" [10–6].[18] Basil Spence, the architect of the winning scheme for Coventry, was moved by his visit to the site: "As soon as I set foot on the ruined nave I felt the impact of delicate enclosure. It was still a cathedral. Instead of the beautiful wooden roof it had skies as a vault."[19] A heroically scaled porch would link the damaged carcass of the old church with his new nave and chapels, a porch to bond the destroyed with the risen.[20] Interestingly, I think, any combination of ruin and modern construction enfolds the seeds of optimism. Together they reflect the crucifixion of Christ and the Resurrection—and the birth of a new completion that triumphs above the derelict architectural fragments. In many ways the progression from the ruin to the altar in the Spence plan outlined a trajectory parallel to that from death to resurrection; like the church's body, the celebrant, too, would experience restoration by following this *via crucis*.[21]

The Sienese had never completed their project for a monumental cathedral and the vestiges of their incomplete effort underscore their civic and economic overreach and ultimate impotence. However, there is a difference between the ruin (which once was) and the incomplete fragment (which has never been). Each tells a differing story of the past: the former tells of a past glory completed; the latter of a hubris that attempted what it could not achieve. In the Berlin and

[10–7]

ADA WILBRAHAM
AND OTHERS,
NINFA GARDENS,
LATINA, ITALY, 1880s+.
[MARC TREIB]

Coventry churches the juxtaposition of old and new forges a symbiosis that draws upon and profits from the qualities of each. But perhaps symbiosis is too strong a term, as no true integration has really been accomplished. Should we look to chemistry for an analogy, the term suspension might prove a better choice than solution. In a solution the chemical elements mix completely to form a new compound. In the suspension —in contrast—the properties of each of the constituents remain inert and identifiable, like unmixed sugar suspended in cold water. The eye—and one might argue the mind as well—rests neither on one nor the other part of these churches. Instead it is lured into a nearly constant play of back and forth, the eternal back and forth of the tennis match without end. The past and the present together—do they suggest a certain future?

Ruins and gardens have long traveled the road together, whether the vegetation has been planted or is volunteer. Set within the ruins of a Roman amphitheater, the gardens of Santa Croce in Gerusaleme complement the religious structure adjacent to them—gardens that produce for the mouth as well as the eye. In the Romantic vision the ruin imbued a sense of history and worth into the garden, as we have seen in the English landscape tradition. At Ninfa, south of Rome, a path of a differing nature was taken [10–7]. Here the deteriorated walls of a medieval city enframed a garden created within

them by the Englishwoman Ada Wilbraham, who began her work in the 1880s.[22] The vision is pastoral despite the site's urban origins, and the omnipresence of vegetation mutes the speech of the ruins, assigning them a subsidiary voice in the theater of the place. The ruin in the park, however, is a far different animal than the park in the ruin, especially when it is an animal of phenomenal scale.

RUINS, REMAINS, AND PARKS

As technology evolves and processes are rendered ineffective or uneconomic, the world is left with extensive zones of industrial waste. The transfer from handcraft to industrialization left relatively little debris in its wake, as the age of handcraft built with organic materials and manufactured materials were employed in relatively limited amounts. Industry, in contrast, built in steel and concrete—and it often built large. But as electronics replaced mechanization, as oil and nuclear power replaced coal and wood, as jobs moved to locations far from the lands of their owners, areas of once vibrant production turned fallow. What should one do with these manufactured sites?

It is said that there are three important factors in selling real estate: location, location, location. And Richard Haag was prescient in understanding that the location of the former gas works in Seattle, Washington, occupied prime real estate. After production stopped in the 1960s there was talk of developing the land—that is, if the toxic byproducts contaminating the soil could be neutralized. Instead Haag designed a park for the site and proposed keeping a portion of the energy-producing equipment as a marker of what had been [10–8, 10–9]. It was a magnificent idea, not easily realized given the state of things and the city's concern for safety and liability. In fact, even after the park was opened problems of toxins continued to plague its use, but over the years Gas Works Park has acquired landmark status in the history of modern landscape architecture.[23]

[10–8]
RICHARD HAAG,
GAS WORKS PARK,
SEATTLE, WASHINGTON,
1978.
[MARC TREIB, 1986]

[10–9]
GAS WORKS PARK,
SEATTLE, WASHINGTON.
[MARC TREIB, 2005]

Some might suggest that the actual experience of being in Gas Works Park is less interesting and engaging than its originating idea. Part of this is due to the nature of remediated terrain and the stringent limits placed upon the planting of trees.[24] In part. But leaving the site open to the sun and wind, and the views, was one of Haag's principal ideas for the park's design. To accomplish that goal, Haag brought in tons of soil —much of it from excavations for high-rise construction downtown—elevating the site by more than 40 feet in the highest areas.[25] The resulting design features a handsomely modeled terrain that culminates in a panoramic outlook, although the landscape lacks any visual complexity or drama beyond that provided by the dramatic vistas. The view and the shoreline are, in fact, the park's main attractions; the reshaped topography and the limited vegetation support movement and a diversity of views. One could argue, in fact, that Haag's principal accomplishment at Gas Works Park was less its specific design and more its very existence—that is, maintaining a fragment of available land as a publicly accessible open space. That in itself is was an epic accomplishment at that time.

The industrial relic from which the park gets its name plays only a small experiential role however, given that for reasons of safety and liability the municipal authorities denied access to the equipment for exploration or play. In terms of semantic consequence, however, this denial may have been positive. The structures are relatively small in relation to the area of the site, and if climbed upon they might lose some of their readings as historical indices. Once meaningful because of their use, in their new role as park attraction they run the risk of being read as neutral structures denuded of significance. As I will return to this thought at the conclusion of the chapter, I will leave Gas Works Park and look at its next major successor, the Landschaftspark Duisburg-Nord in Germany's Ruhr Valley.

So much has been written about this project, and about the attempts to ameliorate the poisoned remnants of industrialization in the Ruhr, that I will skim over the details quickly.[26] From the dawn of industrialization the Ruhr Valley was Germany's primary steel-producing district; indeed, it was one of the major production centers for Europe as a whole. In the 1980s, due primarily to economic challenges from Asian manufacturers, the bottom fell out of the market and the steel plants—as well as the coke facilities that served them— were rendered uneconomical. In 1985 the plants at Duisburg closed; their legacy was a despoiled terrain of gargantuan proportions. The greater industrial wasteland spanned from Duisburg in the west beyond Dortmund in the east—a span of nearly 50 miles. The architectural residue of more than a century of industrial process possessed a heroic scale, colossal machines cast as buildings, or buildings functioning as perfected machines. The earth below these enormous constructions was highly noxious. This was not territory that would calmly return to a natural state on it own, unless the period allowed for self-remediation was measured in millennia rather than years. As humans had ruined the land, it was the human hand that must find some solution to the dereliction and the very threat to human occupation in any form.

Long ago, in his book *The Tourist*, the sociologist Dean MacCannell had argued that the myth that binds industrial, and hence postindustrial, society was that we no longer live the real life in the real place.[27] This unending search for the real and authentic makes us all tourists. We travel and we seek and we look. MacCannell also argued that being divorced from the places from which our food derives—or the places of manufacture for the goods we use—industrial society anxiously strives to learn about what lies behind the scenes of our lives. In rural societies everyone knew where milk and flour came

[10-10] *opposite*
LATZ + PARTNER,
LANDSCHAFTSPARK
DUISBURG-NORD,
DUISBURG-NORD,
GERMANY, 1994+.
[MARC TREIB]

[10-11] *above*
LANDSCHAFTSPARK
DUISBURG-NORD,
DUISBURG-NORD,
GERMANY.
THE EMSCHER CANAL
RESTORED WITH THE
ELEVATED PASSARELLE
TO THE RIGHT.
[MARC TREIB]

[10-12] *below*
LANDSCHAFTSPARK
DUISBURG-NORD,
DUISBURG-NORD,
GERMANY.
OLD CONCRETE
SUPPORTS AND
WALLS NOW USED
FOR RECREATIONAL
CLIMBING.
[MARC TREIB]

from and how and where shoes were made. The factory tour that arose in the nineteenth century was solely the product of the industrial age, deriving from our being distanced and detached from these critical systems of production. In these cultural seeds, perhaps fueled by a romantic tradition, we find the reasons for retaining these relics of industrial production. In some ways their preservation fetishizes them; in other ways, it strips them of their historical meaning.

In 1989 an invited competition was organized by the Internationale Bauaustellung [IBA] to stimulate ideas for transforming almost 500 acres of steel, coke, and coal production into a park. The Landschaftspark Duisburg-Nord was but one small, if highly visible and publicized, part of a broad vision to convert the industrial landscape of the Ruhr into a cultural landscape worthy of a tourist clientele as well as its local population. Latz + Partners' winning scheme retained a significant number of the former steel and coking facilities, a decision based not only on economy but also as a sympathetic regard for the relics of prior times and manufacturing economies [10–10]. Nonetheless, the site would be entirely made over; rumor has it that Peter Latz succeeded in having the site for Duisburg-Nord classified as a wilderness rather than a park, thereby circumventing numerous legal restrictions governing risk and accessibility.[28] Although he had used an almost Jungian image of ravens circling a castle in his competition entry, Latz's rationalism equaled his romanticism. In an early description of the project at an academic symposium, he emphasized that: "This is to become an historical park, but the history starts now and goes forward as well as backwards."[29]

The design strategy was essentially one of reduction, reinterpretation, and overlay. Rather than destroy and clear significant areas of the derelict industrial landscape, the design team demolished, scraped, reused, cleaned, and in places, planted. Volunteer plants and trees accompanied purposeful seedings, and over time much of the site has been covered by flowers and grasses and a succession of trees, primarily birches.

The Emscher Canal has been detoxified, access to it facilitated; aerial walkways support the circulation between the buildings and unimpeded movement between certain areas [10–11]. Didactic machines explain water processing as they clean and aerate the polluted canal. Within the bowels of the concrete bunkers, now in ruins, gardens were planted —gardens curiously polite in their forms and clipped shapes, shapes that contrast mightily against the roughness of the thick-walled structures.

All of this has been described in considerable detail in numerous publications on this unquestionably landmark work. But what has been addressed to a far lesser degree is the basic reason—other than the enormous costs complete demolition would have entailed—just why these industrial structures have been retained. Yes, they represent a manufacturing structure that had long provided the basis for the Ruhr's economy. Yes, they illustrated processes of extraction and production now non-vital and discarded. Yes, we have learned to preserve historic structures as tangible evidence of our past, a collective memory externalized in individual buildings and collectively in cultural landscapes. But one wonders about the precise effect these buildings have on the psyche and memory of the current generation, and will have on those to come. This is the question that vexes any interpretation of Gas Works Park as well.

Behind the practice of preserving structures is the basic premise that they represent our past, and that somehow, they represent us even today. But do they really? There is a reason that we require guides, whether published or human, to explain the past to us. Buildings—sadly perhaps—are stubbornly inarticulate and the stories they have to tell are latent rather than overt. The guide in published form uses photos of active processes and habitation to literally flesh out an image of life within the architecture. The human guide, perhaps clad in period or folk costume, tells us what lives and events took place in this room, a necessary semantic addition to the displays of china and tableware, and perhaps even artificial food, intended to set the stage as well as the table. Of course, it is far easier to imagine past domestic lives than superannuated industrial processes, as production has changed by degree and support rather than in its basic nature. The same is probably true of religion—ritual tends to be perpetuated and rarely suffers radical changes. And perhaps it is unreasonable to demand of colossal industrial structures the same voice of testimony we find, for example, in a church.

But unless we happen to have been the original inhabitants, I believe that we will always require some layer of explanation to make any historical structure or landscape truly relevant. And that layer becomes all the more necessary as the buildings drifts further into the past. That wooden cabin set off from the main house of the plantation—small but nonetheless charming—loses its charm the instant we learn that it housed an incomprehensible number of slaves. The raw beauty of the steel-making structures takes on a rather different aspect when we learn of lives lost and bodies maimed, and the mountains of pollutants it has injected into the soil and the atmosphere. These are the heavy aspects of history not readily evident in the structures themselves. In this sense, the density of history diminishes with time, converting the dimension of semantics into one of nearly pure syntax.

To an eighteenth-century English aristocrat, the ruin was a stimulus for thought, perhaps thought tinged with mood. "A ruin, for instance, may be neither new to us, nor majestick,

[10–13]
KONJIAN YU AND WEI PANG, SHIPYARD PARK, ZHONGSHAN, CHINA, 2002.
[MARC TREIB]

[10–14]
VENTURI & RAUCH, FRANKLIN COURT, PHILADELPHIA, PENNSYLVANIA, 1976.
[MARC TREIB]

nor beautiful," tells William Shenstone, "yet afford that pleasing melancholy which proceeds from a reflexion on decayed magnificence."[30] To the children scaling the concrete columns and walls of Landschaftspark Duisburg-Nord today, these are only concrete columns and walls [10–12]. Yes, they are probably aware that the site once produced steel, and perhaps they have even heard talks trying to educate them about the wealth of their city's past manufacture. But are they really able to vitally experience that which once was? Can their own experience ever approach in intensity and kind the experience of the steelworker who toiled there from 7:00 in the morning to 5:00 in the afternoon each day for 40 years? To that worker the site has a meaning accrued with personal effort, time, and engagement; to the twenty-first-century child meaning accrues in a far different way—it now is a park, after all. In *The Rings of Saturn*, the novelist W. G. Sebald poignantly captured this loss over time:

> But the closer I came to these ruins, the more any notion of a mysterious isle of the dead receded, and the more I imagined myself amidst the remains of our own civilization after its extinction in some future catastrophe. To me too, as for some latter-day stranger ignorant of the nature of our society wandering about among heaps of scrap metal and defunct machinery, the beings who had once lived and worked here were an enigma, as was the purpose of the primitive contraptions and fittings inside the bunkers, the iron rails under the ceilings, the hooks still on the partially tiled walls, the showerheads the size of plates, the ramps and soakaways.[31]

To my mind, these industrial structures—magnificent as they are—are not true ruins. A ruin is a fragment of a whole that somehow, some way, embodies a sense of prior times. Even in its incompleteness the fragment suggests a greater entity once whole. The ruin provokes our memories. It whispers that we should reconsider the past, that we should think about what has been, and perhaps also taunts how we, too, shall be a part of a ruin in times to come. But these industrial structures are remains rather than ruins. A remain, no matter what its dereliction, feels a totality in itself; it satisfies our impression of being complete; it is enough. Now it could just be that it is the enormous scale of these structures that stifles an active engagement with contemplation and any attempts to mentally reconstruct the whole. So vast are these mills that one wonders if they ever could have been any larger, any more complete. How could they? They already stretch to the horizon and terminate only with the vanishing point. As remains, rather than ruins, they ask other questions and they provide other answers. At night a ruin is uncanny and may feel haunted; but at night a remain just feels physically unsafe. The accumulated meaning of history once potent in the remain evaporates rapidly, and in time new meanings accrue to these semantically reduced structures. As Peter Latz said early on, history also starts from today.

How would Caspar David Friedrich have painted the Thyssen steelworks and collieries and cokeries of Duisburg? Given their immense dimensions, they are sublime in themselves, and perhaps he would question only whether they were constructed by a race of giants rather than a race of men.

FRAMEWORKS

Continuing our genealogy of the industrial ruin in the park we now move to China, to the city of Zhongshan, where the landscape architects Konjian Yu and Wei Pang realized the Shipyard Park in 2001.[32] Here the structures have been literally condensed, maintaining their outlines only in sketch form while adapting one or two structures to new uses [10–13]. Much of the site was cleared to create open space and a small lake now modulates water flow while also serving for both visual and recreational pleasure. I am told that several of these outlines were actually new constructions rather than venerable remains, underlining the common practice of ranking syntax over semantics. In that sense new construction can evoke and beg the engagement of the visitor, as does the remain, but rarely to the same degree.

The idea was not a new one. Feeling that the evidence concerning Benjamin Franklin's house in Philadelphia was insufficient for anything beyond a fanciful reconstruction, in 1976 Robert Venturi proposed building only what was known: the mass of the building and its plan (recorded in a letter between the Franklins).[33] The reconstruction blatantly tells us that we do not know much of the pertinent information and, thus, we will present to you only what is known with some degree of certainty [10–14]. Yu and Pang adopted similar thinking when refashioning the frames of the shipbuilding structures. But here, at least in theory, it was an act of selective demolition rather than one of discriminating reconstruction. They then radically changed the context around the structures, in many ways recasting them as follies like those in the English landscape park. One wonders if any former shipyard worker could identify at a deeper level with the place any longer, or whether these remains just tell us that "yes, once there was a shipyard here and the structures were about this large, but yes, there were many more of them, and it was not so pretty."

Perhaps that is all we can ever ask of our industrial remains, no matter how extensive the interpretative programs that accompany their remaking. They are at best markers of times past, structures for current use, and suggestions of how today's today will become soon tomorrow's yesterday no matter how we try to still time.

NOTES

1 For reproductions of Friedrich's paintings see Jens Christian Jensen, *Caspar David Friedrich*, London: Barron's, 1981; William Vaughan, Helmut Börsch-Supan, Hans Joachim Neidhardt, *Caspar David Friedrich, 1774–1840: Romantic Landscape Painting in Dresden*, London: Tate Gallery, 1972; Sabine Rewald, ed., *The Romantic Vision of Caspar David Friedrich: Paintings and Drawings from the U.S.S.R.*, New York: Harry Abrams, 1991.

2 The theme of ruins in art is exhaustively presented in Michel Makarius, *Ruins*, Paris: Flammarion, 2004.

3 The definitive study of this painting remains Erwin Panofsky's "Et in Arcadia Ego: Poussin and the Elegiac Tradition," in *Meaning in the Visual Arts*, Garden City, NY: Doubleday, 1955, pp. 295–320.

4 H. W. Garrod, editor, *The Poetical Works of John Keats*, London: Oxford University Press, 1961, p. 209.

5 Richard Payne Knight, *Analytical Inquiry*, London, 1808, pp. 194–95, quoted in Tom Turner, *English Garden Design: History and Styles since 1650*, Woodbridge, UK: Antique Collectors' Club, 1986, p. 122.

6 See John Dixon Hunt, *Garden and Grove: The Italian Renaissance Garden in the English Imagination, 1600–1750*, Philadelphia: University of Pennsylvania Press, 1996.

7 George Clark, Jonathan Marsden, Richard Wheeler, Michael Bevington, and Tim Knox, *Stowe Landscape Gardens*, Swindon, UK: National Trust, 1987.

8 "Of the six hundred and fifty monasteries in England seized by Henry VIII in the 1530s, a third have disappeared under grass." Christopher Woodward, *In Ruins*, London: Vintage, 2002, p. 108. On Fountains Abbey and Studley Royal, see Mary Mauchline and Lydia Greeves, *Fountains Abbey & Studley Royal*, no city: National Trust, 1988.

9 See Diana Ketchum, *Le Désert de Retz: An Eighteenth-Century French Folly Garden*, Cambridge, Mass.: MIT Press, 1994; and Dora Wiebenson, *The Picturesque Garden in France*, Princeton, NJ: Princeton University Press, 1978.

10 John Brinckerhoff Jackson examines this subject in detail in "The Necessity for Ruins," in *The Necessity for Ruins and Other Topics*, Amherst: University of Massachusetts Press, 1980, pp. 89–102.

11 For a discussion of re-use and the transformation of intended meaning, see Jas Elsner, "Iconoclasm and the Preservation of Memory," in Robert S. Nelson and Margaret Olin, eds, *Monuments and Memory,*

Made and Unmade, Chicago: University of Chicago Press, 2003, pp. 209–231.

12 For the story of the competition and the construction of the final design see Kristin Feireiss, Egon Eiermann: *Die Kaiser-Wilhelm-Gedächtnis-Kirche*, Berlin: Ernst & Sohn, 1994.

13 Annemarie Jaeggi, editor, *Egon Eiermann (1904–1970): Die Kontinuität der Moderne*, Karlsruhe: Städtische Galerie, 2005, p. 51. I thank Judith Stilgenbauer for translating these materials.

14 Eiermann: "If through the spontaneously expressed will of the people of Berlin the requirements have changed, the solution must also change." Ibid., p. 52.

15 "I can't atttribute meaning to the ruin of the tower; thus I can't make it a part of the new church," said Eiermann. "I will leave the tower in place as it is ... I can not bring new life to it. It will remain dead." Ibid., p. 56

16 Eiermann had proposed from the start to incorporate the masonry rubble of the historical church within the body of the new building. But it seems he wanted to completely destroy any possible reading of the material as historic architecture. Ibid., p. 52. Le Corbusier had employed a similar strategy in his design for the chapel of Nôtre Dame de Ronchamp in France, building the chapel's massive walls from an old structure destroyed in the war. On Ronchamp and the ideas behind its form see Le Corbusier, *Le livre de Ronchamp*, Paris: Les Cahiers Forces Vives, 1961.

17 "The existing tower is to be retained, either separate or as part of the new Cathedral." *Schedule of Requirements and Accommodation* [Competition Program], included as Appendix B, Basil Spence, *Phoenix at Coventry: The Building of a Cathedral*, London: Fontana Books, 1964, p. 126.

18 "Together with cultural luminaries, including T. S. Eliot and John Maynard Keynes, [Clark] signs a letter to The Times on 15 August 1944 proposing that a number of bombed churches should be preserved in ruins as war memorials. They would be monuments to the mood of the Blitz, and would stand to remind a new generation of 'the sacrifice on which [their] apparent security has been built'." Woodward, *In Ruins*, p. 212. Woodward also describes the British program for war artists— which had also recorded the horrors of the First World War—and the publication of the book *Bombed Churches as War Memorials*, (no author), The Architectural Press, 1945.

19 Basil Spence, *Phoenix at Coventry*, p. 18.

20 For a pictorial tour of Coventry Cathedral see H. C. N Williams, *A Guide to Coventry Cathedral and its Ministry*, London: Hodder and Stoughton, 1966.

21 See Louise Campbell, "Shaping the sacred: Spence as a church-builder," in (no editor), *Basil Spence, Architect*, Edinburgh: National Galleries of Scotland, 2007, pp. 63–76.

22 Woodward, *In Ruins*, pp. 77–82.

23 For background on Richard Haag and the Gas Works Park see Jory Johnson and Felice Frankel, *Modern Landscape Architecture: Redefining the Garden*, New York: Abbeville Press, 1991, pp. 199–208; William Saunders, ed., *Richard Haag: Bloedel Reserve and Gas Works Park*, New York: Princeton Architectural Press, 1998, especially pp. 61–72; and "It Was a Real Gas," *Progressive Architecture*, November 1978, pp. 96–99.

24 At the time of construction, engineering norms required toxic soil to be capped and that no tree roots be allowed to penetrate that clay layer—ruptures could support the infiltration of pollutants. Haag explains the logic behind his design in Luzia Pirzio-Biroli, "Adaptive Re-use, Layering of Meaning on Sites of Industrial Ruin," *Arcade*, Winter 2004, pp. 28–31.

25 Interview with Rich Haag, 14 August 2008, Seattle.

26 Among the publications on the Ruhr project as a whole and the Landschaftspark

Duisburg-Nord in particular are: *Internationale Bauaustellung Emscher Park, Katalog Der Projekte 1999, Internationale Bauaustellung Emscher Park,* no city given, 1999; Brenda Brown, "Reconstructing the Ruhrgebiet," *Landscape Architecture,* 4, 2001; Matt Steinglass, "The Machine in the Garden," *Metropolis,* Oct, 2000; Udo Weilacher, *Between Landscape Architecture and Art,* Basel: Birkhaüser, 1999, pp. 121–136; "Duisburg North Landscape Park," *Anthos,* March 1992, pp. 27–32; Peter Latz, "Landscape Park Duisburg-Nord: The Metamorphosis of an Industrial Site," in Niall Kirkwood, ed., *Manufactured Sites: Rethinking the Post-Industrial Landscape,* London: Spon Press, 2001, pp. 150–161; on its vegetation: *Industriernatur im Land-schaftspark Duisburg-Nord,* Duisburg: Landschaftspark Duisburg-Nord, 1999; on the art program for the Emscher Park: Bernhard Mensch and Peter Pachnicke, eds, *Routenführer Landmarken-Kunst,* Oberhausen: IBA Emscher Park, 1999.

27 Dean MacCannell, *The Tourist: A New Theory of the Leisure Class,* New York: Schocken Books, 1976.

28 I have never been able to confirm this story however, and it may be apocryphal.

29 Peter Latz, "'Design' by Handling the Existing," in Martin Knuijt, Hans Ophuis, and Peter van Saane, eds, *Modern Park Design: Recent Trends,* Bussum, Netherlands: Thoth Publishers, 1995, p. 91.

30 William Shenstone, "Unconnected Thoughts on Gardening," in John Dixon Hunt and Peter Willis, *The Genius of the Place: The English Garden, 1680–1820,* Cambridge, Mass.: MIT Press, 1975, p. 289.

31 W. G. Sebald, *The Rings of Saturn,* trans. Michael Hulse, New York: New Directions, 1998, p. 237.

32 A presentation of factual and background information on the project is found in Kongjian Yu and Mary Padua, eds, *The Art of Survival: Recovering Landscape Architecture,* Mulgrave, Australia: Images Publishing Group, 2006, pp. 138–161. Padua provides an interpretative essay on the park in the same publication, pp. 162–166. See also Mary Padua, "Industrial Strength," *Landscape Architecture,* June 2003, pp. 76–85, 105–107.

33 The house was built 1763–1765, but Franklin spent little time there, serving on various diplomatic missions for almost 20 years. Although there is little text, for images of Franklin Court see David Dunster, ed., *Venturi and Rauch: The Public Buildings,* London: Academy Editions, pp. 80–83; and David Brownlee, David de Long, and Kathryn Hiesinger, *Out of the Ordinary: Robert Venturi, Denise Scott Brown and Associates, Architecture, Urban Design, Design,* Philadelphia: Philadelphia Museum of Art, 2001, pp. 69–71.

[11]
The Memory Industry and its Discontents: The Death and Life of a Keyword

Andrew Shanken

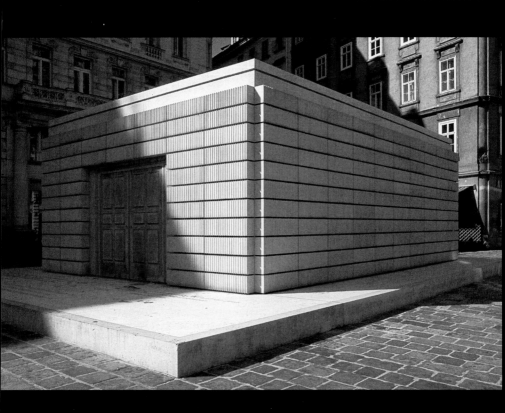

In times of revolution and cultural upheaval, memorials often become victims of political iconoclasm or cultural revisionism. In nineteenth-century Paris, the fall of the Soviet Union, and with the end of Saddam Hussein's rule in Iraq, memorials were pulled down as conspicuous symbols of despised regimes. Recently a more subtle irritation with memorials has entered public discourse that curiously has nothing to do with these more dramatic turns in history. "Too Many Memorials?" a journalist asked in 2007, bemoaning the banality of the recent spate of memorials across Europe [11–1, 11–2].[1] Also in the United States, a kind of memorial exhaustion has set in, with parallels in academia, where references to memory have become ubiquitous in the humanities and social sciences. During the last generation, memory has become one of the keywords of our times, but its sources and its rather contentious journey, even over the past two decades, remain underexamined. Too often memory—the keyword—and its material manifestation —the memorial—have been combed from their cultural braid and treated separately. This chapter explores memory's emergence as a keyword in the context of important memorials and conventions in memorialization.

AMASSING MEMORY

Even amid what now appears to be an overworked field, one finds a host of new books on memory and memorials that use a range of new methods and produce an endless stream of conferences—all of which signals increasing popular interest.[2] The study of the neurological workings of memory is still in its infancy. Someday, perhaps soon, hard science will bequeath to the humanities a trove of material. Outside of academia, memory has also flourished. The endless media treatment of the site of the former World Trade Center, the succession of tragedies—from Oklahoma City and Columbine to Hurricane Katrina, the Tsunami of 2004, and the Iraq War—have piled up events that call out for commemoration.

This surfeit of "memory" is not without its problems. Even in a mass society, with billions of rememberers to go around, events have placed heavy demands on the commemorative machinery of our day. Part of the issue is that modern, pluralistic societies are polytheistic—they do not adhere to

[11–1]
RACHEL WHITEREAD,
HOLOCAUST MEMORIAL,
VIENNA, AUSTRIA, 2005.
[MARC TREIB]

[11-2]
PETER EISENMAN,
HOLOCAUST
MEMORIAL, BERLIN,
GERMANY, 2005.
[MARC TREIB]

unified conventions or rituals: each new loss demands a new act of collective creativity and the invention of new modes of commemoration. This is the consequence on a mass scale of the changing attitudes towards death brilliantly exposed by Philippe Ariès in *Hour of Our Death*.[3] To Ariès, by the mid-twentieth century death had replaced sex as the central taboo of Western society, quarantined in institutions like hospitals and funeral parlors (the word parlor, from the French *parler*, to talk, points out the irony of these places, where people do anything but talk). The result is that death has been hushed out of the home and excised from the public sphere. What is true for individual loss may also hold true for collective loss. A world without commonly accepted practices for responding to collective loss must constantly negotiate new methods.

At the same time, a world of six billion people joined by a global economy and mass media experiences loss on an unprecedented scale, with ubiquitous access through television, radio, and the Internet. Not only do we now live in a world of trauma without borders, but also we simply have experienced tragedy, mourning, and loss more publicly—and at the same time, we are less equipped to handle it. To take one example, the World Trade Center towers didn't fall once on 11 September 2001; they fell thousands of times that day and in the weeks that followed, as news channels looped the most dramatic images over their coverage. How would Americans create a counter-image? Would leaders attempt to create an "iconography of revenge?" Would they stage an act of equal and opposite destruction to satiate the vengeance and bloodlust of the public? In an event so given over to the media, mourning becomes visual, but the ramifications of this for memorialization remain incompletely explored. To put this in demographic terms, the supply of commemoration—a creative, energetic activity—has failed to keep pace with the rate of human destruction. The pace stymies efforts to create new mnemonics that might stabilize the meaning of that destruction in vital social figures like memorials, or even in memorial debate. These are the circumstances that led to the institutionalization of memory practices and the rise of the keyword.

MEMORY AS A KEYWORD

In coining the term "memory industry" in the year 2000, the Berkeley historian Kerwin Klein intended to suggest something of the rationalization of memory as an object of inquiry, an inquiry that ranged from the museum trade and the obsession in academia over the past 25 years to genealogy, the abrupt rise of recovered memories, and the legal battles surrounding them.[4] We might add to his short list the rise of the heritage industry in the United States and the ongoing multiplication of World Heritage sites around the world, a practice which might be seen as the exportation and globalization of Western memory traditions and values.

The context of Klein's article is important, as conditions have intensified over time. He was writing in the United States —one of the engines of the memory industry—at the turn of the millennium, after, importantly, the fall of the Soviet Union, the fiftieth anniversaries of the end of World War II and the Holocaust, and in academia, the thorough dissemination of structuralism, post-structuralism, and that loose group of wry, neurotic, and often disintegrative tendencies called post-modernism. Memory, it seemed to Klein, had become a "metahistorical category" that subsumed a range of other terms, including history itself. It owed its power, he claimed, to the way it "marries hip new linguistic practices with some of the oldest senses of memory as a union of divine presence and material object."[5] Klein's article appeared in a special issue of *Representations* devoted to memory, the second in eleven years for that journal. The issue was, unavoidably, part of the memory industry, as was Klein himself—a small irony considering that Pierre Nora had first articulated his famous concept of the *lieux de mémoire* (sites of memory) in the same journal in 1989, explicitly opposing history and memory.[6]

Nora's work, as much as any, provided the intellectual touchstone for memory studies. While Maurice Halbwachs and Henri Bergson are often credited with the first important work on the subject, Nora's *lieux de mémoire* helped spawn a subfield and brought memory to light as a keyword. Nora's thesis posed a paradox, however: history, understood as the rationalization and institutionalization of the past, had destroyed the purported organic ways in which pre-modern cultures remember, extracting them from daily practices for safe-keeping in archives, museums, books, plaques, and the like—in other words, exchanging people for institutions. Modern history had killed pre-modern memory. The reasoning closely parallels Ariés's coeval work on death, but Nora's work was instrumental and socially engaged. The *lieux de mémoire* were supposed to save memory from history by creating a category in between the two, safeguarded from the mysticism of the first and girded against the stultifying rationality of the second. It remained unclear, however, how Nora's history would be so radically different from the history he claimed had killed the culture of memory that he so wished to resurrect. The concept of the *lieux de mémoire* was predicated, in other words, on the irrational proposition that memory existed as a social force that possessed different properties than history. As it arose as a keyword in the late twentieth century, memory was pitched against the highly constructed nature of history as part of a nostalgic effort to reclaim premodern traditions.[7]

Klein's phrase dissolved this myth, revealing the institutionalization of memory, at least within the academy, and it did so at a key moment in the transformation of memory studies. Klein was writing in 1999, when the entire world seemed perched on the precipice of millennium destruction, as the days ground towards Y2K. While most of modernity, and even post-modernity, had been wrestling with the acceleration of events—or to use another trendy and romanticized word "time"—Y2K threatened to make the clocks stand still. How could a world that had seemingly been accelerating since the Industrial Revolution be struck static by a computer glitch, and a calendrical one at that? Y2K, after all, was the year in which the future was supposed to begin: the target date of the future, its embodiment, for at least a century. If you came to consciousness before, say, 1984, you remember hearing of the glorious world in which we would eat pills instead of food, push buttons instead of work, fly in personal flivving fliers, and live with hundreds of other prophesies that originated with Jules Verne and H. G. Wells and thereafter popularized by advertisements, popular science magazines, and world's fairs. With the approach of the millennium the fears of computer malfunction leading to blackouts, traffic chaos, the destruction of the credit system, malfeasance of all sorts as alarms went haywire, and perhaps the launching of nuclear warheads sucked the future out of the trope of the year 2000. Y2K involved one tick of the clock: future and past fell out of sight, at least temporarily. While this was not memory's moment here was *Representations* hot on its trail.

The following September witnessed the destruction of the World Trade Center, catapulting memory into popular consciousness on a new scale while cutting new rhetorical contours for the keyword. But when and under what conditions had this keyword emerged in the first place? Memory did not appear as an entry in Raymond Williams's important compendium *Keywords* of 1976. Williams's book canonized the keywords approach, asserting that "important social and historical processes occur within language," embedded in neologisms or new uses of old words, in their adaptation, alteration, extension, or transfer, as well as in the co-existence of contrary or conflicted meanings.[8] Language for Williams was a form of hidden history, a well-worn practice for philologists looking at ancient words, but neglected in the study of recent history. Tracing modernity's keywords would reveal some of the nuanced shifts in consciousness of the modern period.

Memory stands apart from Williams's bundle of keywords that shaped the revolutionary changes of the industrial and political revolutions that altered the world between 1776 and the early twentieth century. His core words—art, industry, class, democracy, and foremost, culture—all changed meaning in this period, and launched a series of other modern usages and neologisms, including bureaucracy, rationalism, utilitarian, speculation, capitalism, and communism, to name only a few. Memory did not belong among these seminal descriptions of the modern world, in part because its roots extend further back in time. As Frances Yates's book *The Art of Memory* demonstrated, memory played a central part in Roman rhetoric; it was foundational to medieval Christian concepts of virtue and vice; and Renaissance humanists carried it through their memory theaters until, as Yates claimed, it helped forge the scientific method of modern society.[9] Moreover most commemorative practices and conventions have ancient, or at very least medieval, roots. When we jump from the word to the physical memorial itself, the same holds true. Most contemporary memorials lean on long-standing habits. Even those that seem to be great departures from the past turn out to be creative revisions. Maya Lin's oft-cited Vietnam Memorial, for example, builds on an ancient tradition of walls with names, and fires up the emotional intensity with changes in elevation, reflection, and other means.

The point is that memory eluded Raymond Williams because neither the word, nor practices associated with it, were modern. In fact, the word memory may have been anathema to the secularizing mood of the eighteenth and nineteenth centuries, where Frances Yates's account of the art of memory abruptly ends. At roughly the same time that Americans ushered in the political revolutions of modernity, a Congressman dismissed memorials as "good for nothing," and John Quincy Adams, a son of the Revolution, declared that "democracy has no monuments."[10] Few American towns had memorials until long after Reconstruction. On the other side of the temporal arc of the modern world, in 1938—

in the midst of the greatest retreat of industrial capitalism of the twentieth century—Lewis Mumford pronounced that the notion of a modern monument was a contradiction: "If it is a monument," he famously wrote, "it is not modern."[11] Memory, it seems, was not a fundamental part of the same Enlightenment forces that radically reshaped the world in the nineteenth and twentieth centuries, despite the legion of memorials constructed in those years. This leaves an awkward disparity between the dismissive secularity of modernity and the concurrent proliferation of memorials: the first blocked memory from becoming a keyword, while the second erected would-be *aide-mémoires* in every city and town in Europe and America.

How is it that memory did not make it into Raymond Williams' *Keywords* in 1976, but is now such an overheated topic that scholars like Klein package it in apt but cynical terms like the "memory industry?" The answer lies in a number of discontents that are lodged in the trajectory of history since World War II. Raymond Williams is again instructive here, as much for couching the argument in generational terms, as for his intellectual contribution. When he returned to London in 1945 after fighting in the war, he noticed a change in what he called the "new and strange world" that he had re-entered, concluding: "they just don't speak the same language."[12] The war had altered the conditions of life, thereby changing language. The new language, Williams quickly realized, represented some fundamentally changed attitudes. In turn, that new language altered the conditions of life. Over the next 30 years, as he collected material for *Keywords*, memory continued to elude Williams's lexicon.

Oddly, on the other side of the Atlantic in 1945, a heated debate broke out about post-war memorials. Even before the war ended, Americans argued over the way the nation should memorialize the war, with one side advocating purely commemorative memorials like arches, obelisks, and columns, while the other side called for living or useful memorials like community centers, parks, gymnasiums, and highways. Williams may have missed this debate given that conditions in Britain were quite different, and he slanted his keywords strongly towards British sources. But on the American homefront the word memorial was everywhere, at least for a brief moment—and then, curiously, it disappeared. In fact, memorials ran so counter to the utilitarian spirit after World War II that Americans denigrated traditional ones as indulgent, vulgar, useless, or dead—some of the same terms used 50 years later to dismiss the National Memorial to World War II in Washington, D.C.[13] In fact, few iconic memorials emerged out of World War II in the United States. The soldiers who fought the war grew laconic about their experiences, and Holocaust survivors habitually refused to talk about their painful ordeal. As Paul Fussell observed, World War II, unlike the first one, failed to produce a great literature. The same may be said about its effect on memorials. The fact that the United States took over 50 years to build a national memorial to this war in Washington, D.C. is ample proof that some form of memorial exhaustion set in [11–3].

Aside from the Soviet Bloc's Stalinmania, much of Europe experienced a similar response [11–4]. The additive plaques and other addenda to memorials from this war provide further proof. Instead of erecting a second memorial to the Royal Fusiliers who died in World War II, for example, Londoners added only a short text to the World War I memorial on the Strand in London. To avoid the same problem recurring in the future, they cut out some stone and added a second pro-vision—rather like taking out an insurance policy: "those fusiliers killed in subsequent campaigns." [11–5] No one will ever have to propose or reject another Royal Fusiliers memorial again. In the twentieth century, memory—like its cousin, death—has carried some of the qualities of a social taboo, yet another reason why Williams may have overlooked it.

The late twentieth century has challenged all of this. Nora's work, the beginnings of Holocaust studies, and the controversies over the Vietnam Memorial in Washington in the early 1980s awakened an interest among scholars in memory and memorials. From there it entered the lexicon, appearing in the critical extension to Williams's work pub-lished in 2005, *The New Keywords*. There it was bundled with heritage, Holocaust, and time—all new additions.[14]

MEMORY AND MULTICULTURALISM

What had been a taboo as recently as a generation ago has today become thoroughly institutionalized.[15] The fate of the Vietnam Memorial brings this point home. Although well-known, the story bears repeating: in part because so much of the scholar-ship on memory continues to argue through this memorial, but also because it demonstrates a little-observed yet fundamen-tal change that drove memory as a keyword in the 1980s and 1990s. Maya Lin's spare black granite wall brought memorials up to date with developments in art [11–6, 11– 7]. Not sur-prisingly, it incited instant controversy. Shortly after its completion in 1982, disgruntled veterans demanded a more figurative memorial. Calling Lin's design a black gash and a negative critique of the war, they campaigned for a more affirming memorial: code for a conventional piece.

In response, Frederick Hart completed a figurative work in 1984, a rapid-fire retort in the slow-moving world

[11–3] *above*
FRIEDRICH ST. FLORIAN,
UNITED STATES
NATIONAL WORLD
WAR II MEMORIAL,
WASHINGTON, D.C.,
2004.
[ANDREW SHANKEN]

[11–4] *below left*
ALBERT TOFT,
ROYAL FUSILIERS'
MEMORIAL,
LONDON, 1921.
[ANDREW SHANKEN]

[11–5] *below right*
ADDITION TO THE
ROYAL FUSILIERS'
MEMORIAL, LONDON.
[ANDREW SHANKEN]

AND THOSE FUSILIERS
KILLED IN SUBSEQUENT CAMPAIGNS

of memorials. [11–8, 11–9]. Three soldiers, each ethnically different, gaze mournfully at Lin's wall, as if looking at their fallen brethren. Lin's design is controlled and open-ended. By contrast, Hart's maudlin statues leave little room for interpretation or spontaneous commemorative practices. The soldiers return to what Philippe Ariès has called the "ostentatious" mourning of the nineteenth century. Simultaneously, they offer an artistic commentary on the abstraction and restraint of Lin's memorial.

In art historical terms, the dialog between Lin's and Hart's memorials signals the passing of an era of legible, unequivocal artistic traditions. In place of the supposed universality of classicism, of figural narration or allegory in art, Lin's design taps into the universality of abstraction. Reflections in the granite, descent into the v-shaped trough, and the seemingly infinite rows of names: these become the triggers of pathos that rise above history and culture—or so proponents of abstraction would believe. Enter the war-torn men in fatigues whose realism recalls an artistic dilemma almost a century old by the 1980s.[16]

Memorials have had a fitful time with emerging art movements in the twentieth century. Until recently few American memorials in the decades following World War II relied on avant-garde art. The dilemma of post-war memorialization derived not only from the emergence of useful memorials and the decline of the figurative tradition. It also encountered the new directions taken by art in the post-war decades. With the turn to abstract expressionism, to pop and conceptual art, artists had turned their backs on the wellspring of commemorative art: those tropes and allegories that European society had elaborated since the Middle Ages expressly for memorial purposes—first out of the central death of Christianity and later out of its growing cast of saints and martyrs.

[11–6]
MAYA LIN,
VIETNAM VETERANS
MEMORIAL,
WASHINGTON, D.C.,
1982.
[MARC TREIB]

[11–7]
VIETNAM VETERANS
MEMORIAL,
WASHINGTON, D.C.
[MARC TREIB]

Among these post-war movements, minimalism stands out. Already pedigreed by the early 1980s, Lin was the first to willfully apply minimalism to the design of memorials , and not merely as an aesthetic of simplicity born of the dehistoricizing urges of the modern movement in architecture. Lin's move struck a chord in part because of the political context in which it occurred. As the most contentious issue of the day the Vietnam War was fought alongside social unrest and protest, part of the same set of forces that liberalized American society and led to multiculturalism as well as the Cold War. Minimalism arose in the same years and gave a wide berth to these multiple viewpoints. It is an art that is assertive with space, not meaning. It sets a stage but leaves it empty for the spectator, who participates as an actor in the construction of meaning. Minimalism's impatience with abstract expressionism transcended a distrust of the artistic, the fussy, and the inner life of the artist, to disengage with the rigid encounter between the work of art on a wall and the adoring or bored viewer in a museum. Lin used minimalism to restore some of the possibility of the cairn, boulder, or burial mound, those most ancient memorial traditions that transform landscape or liken the unfathomable forces and eons behind the appearance of an erratic boulder in a landscape to a life and its loss. The inconclusiveness of the Vietnam War and the upheaval associated with it lent themselves to such a vocabulary. The multiculturalism born of the same social forces would demand still a different one.

By the time Lin's memorial was finished multiculturalism had drifted from the rarefied academy to the vitiated air of popular culture—and figuration had returned in art. Hart's group is probably the first evidence of multiculturalism making its way into a memorial. The ethnic variety of his soldiers was assumed, an insipid attempt to bronze a matter that demands a deeper rethinking of the memorial tradition as well

[11-8]
FREDERICK HART, SCULPTOR; *THREE SERVICEMEN*, VIETNAM VETERANS MEMORIAL, WASHINGTON, D.C., 1984.
[LIBRARY OF CONGRESS, PRINTS AND PHOTOGRAPHS DIVISION, HISTORIC AMERICAN BUILDINGS]

[11-9]
THREE SERVICEMEN, VIETNAM VETERANS MEMORIAL, WASHINGTON, D.C..
[LIBRARY OF CONGRESS, PRINTS AND PHOTOGRAPHS DIVISION, HISTORIC AMERICAN BUILDINGS]

as cultural difference. After all, by the 1980s even advertising had taken to what we can now identify as the United Colors of Benetton (begun 1982), the marketing of racial or ethnic variety [11–10]. There were precedents: the Iwo Jima Memorial also represented multiple ethnicities, but this reflected the actual soldiers who staked the flag atop Mount Suribachi. Frederick Hart's memorial, by contrast, is a fiction driven by a political agenda, an agenda we may very well agree with while ruing the trespass on Lin's memorial. The problem is that figuration returned in the 1980s in the form of a post-modern critique, a suitable mode for commenting on the Vietnam War, while Hart's sculpture is anything but ironic. This nudges the figures of the soldiers towards kitsch.

Washington thus received two Vietnam Memorials. The first was a breakthrough in solving the dilemma of figuration in memorials. It became an instant icon but it resisted using icons. This restraint made the second memorial by Hart appear to be even more a *retarditaire* exercise. Their confrontation neatly reveals the contradiction inherent in the era that nurtured both liberal political correctness and the conservative family values. Had the story ended there, Hart's soldiers would be an awkward footnote, but the Vietnam War has led to the shaping of a memorial precinct on the Mall in which an ongoing conversation about matters other than Vietnam continues.

[11–10]
CLOTHING
ADVERTISEMENT,
BENETTON, ITALY,
1985.
[OLIVIERO TOSCANI,
© COPYRIGHT 1985
BENETTON GROUP
S.P.A.]

More memorials would come. Hart's memorial represented three men mourning the loss of mostly male combatants. Women, too, had played an important role in the war: 11,500 of them served overseas. They, too, needed a place on the Mall. The Vietnam Women's Memorial (1993), a sentimental handmaiden's tale of a memorial on a peripheral site, expresses a marginal role for women in Vietnam [11-11]. It is so clearly addenda, a perverse disservice to the very point of multicultural sensitivity.

Now when tourists and schoolchildren on field trips visit the site, the social script is set: a lost war, proud veterans, under-represented women—all set in a landscape whose power is dissipated by unplanned commemorative accumulation. In the effort to steer memorials away from the overly heroic and assertive language of traditional memorials such as the Washington or Lincoln Memorials (obelisk and temple, respectively), the opposite problem has emerged: memorial babble.

THE MEMORIAL INDUSTRY AND OVERPRODUCTION

Even more recently, the immaturity or impetuousness of commemoration in the age of political correctness has been revealed. Congress is currently considering a Vietnam Veterans Memorial Center that would offer interpretive material for the increasing number of people who have no direct connection with the war, or even with the conflicts surrounding the memorials. The new building, in order to respond sensitively to the site, would be dug out entirely behind Lin's wall. A glass curtain wall would open into a two-storied exhibition hall filled with the spontaneous offerings left at the wall, exhibitions with the faces keyed to names on the wall, and other educational exhibitions. Outside, a reflecting pool with glass sculptural tubes would fill a small court that connects the axis of the memorial with the Center. This new piece would constitute a fourth intervention on the site. As James S. Russell has written: "Even buried buildings don't disappear, and if the center's purpose is meaningful, it needs to be visible and expressed."[17] The interpretive center, part of a current vogue in memorial design, is an admission of failure. It points out the rapid obsolescence of these memorials—the last not even 15 years old.

As a point of comparison: the Lincoln Memorial is entering into its ninth decade [11–12]. Over time it has been reinvested with meaning by, among other things, the Civil Rights marches that are historically linked with Vietnam War protest (and without the aid of a vast interpretive center).[18] Why is it that the more recent Vietnam Memorial cannot remain as vivid? It seems as if we have entered a historical middle ground in which the sharp emotion associated with the Vietnam War has ebbed, but with insufficient time for a rich co-option of the memorial for other purposes. One wonders,

[11–12]
HENRY BACON,
LINCOLN MEMORIAL,
WASHINGTON, D.C.,
1922.
[MARC TREIB]

however, if the scattered form of the Vietnam landscape in Washington, D.C. will unintentionally fix boundaries around its meaning. For all of their supposed faults, monumental, heroic works like the Lincoln Memorial make easy targets for appropriation. The meaning of icons comes and goes but they remain icons nonetheless: visible landmarks that are well known and therefore highly sought after as stages for social and political struggle. Will the same be true for the Vietnam memorials? Its lesson seems to be that we can only build our way out of forgetting if we never stop building.

The effects of this approach, judging by the Vietnam assemblage and the growing population of memorials on the Mall, will not be known for many years. But it has established a pattern for memorial design most evident at the Korean War Memorial (1995), its pendant on the Mall [11–13]. As if to forestall the conflicts of the Vietnam War Memorial, the Korean War counterpart came pre-packaged as an aggregate affair: a compilation of wall, figurative elements, fountain, and a vertical accent. In addition to the names, garish, poorly scaled faces are bitten into the stone. The embarrassingly bad likenesses appear like shrunken heads next to the reflections of the visitors. The simple and direct sense of movement in Lin's masterpiece is lost amid the debris of the Korean War Memorial. All of the problems associated with the traditional

[11–13]
FRANK GAYLORD, SCULPTOR; COOPER-LECKY, ARCHITECTS; KOREAN WAR MEMORIAL, WASHINGTON, D.C., 1995.
[MARC TREIB]

memorial—namely that it was useless, vulgar, indulgent, and dead—have returned with the Korean War Memorial. Even the haunting, over-scaled soldiers who walk tensely in a "field" by the wall lose their gravitas: signage tells us not to walk with them—the very thing we ought to be doing. As a whole, it is a one-man band of a memorial, playing almost every memorial convention loudly, but playing none of them well.

These examples point out a crisis. As the Mall in Washington, D.C. fills, so do our personal calendars with days of remembrance, mourning, and commemoration. Many towns and cities face a similar dilemma to the nation's capital. The burden is on informal practices to absorb the stream of new commemorative demands. Soon, in fact, we may experience a threshing—perhaps official conventions will arise for putting to rest old memorials and memorial days—as our spaces and calendars become saturated with mnemonics that undermine the way a mnemonic works in the first place. Every culture with longevity must expunge or become threatened with constant commemorative obligations.

The exhaustion surrounding memory may come out of this impending crisis of commemoration. Spontaneous memorials, or what we might call short-term memorials, would allow temporary observation; if, through sustained practice, people drive the short-term memory into a long-term memory, then a permanent memorial would likely follow—as is sometimes the case. Vladimir Lenin proposed just this sort of process in Soviet Russia after 1919, erecting statues of plaster, clay, and plywood; only those acclaimed by the masses would find their way to bronze and marble.[19] In the United States, the recent spate of impromptu memorials, not just on roadsides, but elsewhere, suggests such a change, a higher, more public profile for the practice, if not the beginnings of a new twist on the tradition.

In fact, we might question the very premise that memorials ought to be permanent, to historicize this urge. Is it just we moderns, with our fingers on the stopwatch and memory leaking out of our calendars and archives, or Blackberries and computers—is it only we who demand permanence? After all, Mnemosyne, the mother of the Greek muses, never required permanence of her creative daughters.

NOTES

1 Jonathan Jones, "Too Many Memories?" *The Guardian*, 26 January 2007.

2 *Time* magazine examined the nature of memory in its issue of 29 January 2007.

3 Philippe Ariès, *The Hour of Our Death*, trans. Helen Weaver, New York: Vintage Books, 1981.

4 Kerwin Lee Klein, "On the Emergence of Memory in Historical Discourse," *Representations* 69 (2000), p. 127.

5 Ibid., p. 129.

6 Pierre Nora, "Between Memory and History: *Les Lieux de Mémoire*," *Representations* 26 (1989), pp. 7–25.

7 Stephen Legg, "Contesting and Surviving Memory: Space, Nation, and Nostalgia," *Environment and Planning Design: Society and Space* 23 (2005), pp. 481–504.

8 Raymond Williams, *Keywords: A Vocabulary of Culture and Society*, revised edition, New York: Oxford University Press, 1983, p. 22. The approach has attracted some of the finest historians. See especially Eric Hobsbawm, *The Age of Revolution*, New York: New American Library, 1962, and Daniel Rodgers, *Contested Truths: Keywords in American Politics since Independence*, New York: Basic Books Inc., 1987.

9 Frances A. Yates, *Art of Memory*, 1966, reprint London: Pimlico, 2001.

10 Kirk Savage, "History, Memory, and Monuments: An Overview of the Scholarly Literature on Commemoration," http://www.cr.nps.gov/history/resedu/savage.htm, accessed 14 April 2008.

11 Lewis Mumford, *The Culture of Cities*, New York: Harcourt, Brace, Jovanovich, 1938, p. 438.

12 Williams, p. 11. This observation was shared by the American Paul Fussell who colorfully demonstrated how World War II had ushered in a new language. Paul Fussell, *Wartime: Understanding and Behavior in the Second World War*, New York: Oxford University Press, 1989.

13 For the general terms of this debate, see Andrew M. Shanken, "Planning Memory: The Rise of Living Memorials in the United States during World War II," *Art Bulletin* (March 2002), pp. 130–147. Even before World War I, an opponent of the proposed Lincoln Memorial denigrated Henry Bacon's classical design by calling it dead. See Christopher A. Thomas, *The Lincoln Memorial & American Life*, Princeton, NJ: Princeton University Press, 2002.

14 Tony Bennett, Lawrence Grossberg, et al., *The New Keywords: A Revised Vocabulary of Culture and Society*, Malden, Mass.: Blackwell Publishing, 2005.

15 The following section reworks arguments first presented in Andrew M. Shanken, "Memento More: Putting the New Wave of Memorials into Context," *Frameworks* (Fall, 2005).

16 Horatio Greenough faced similar problems with his bare-chested George Washington as an enthroned Roman emperor (1833–1836), now on display in the Museum of American History because it embarrassed visitors to the rotunda of the Capitol building.

17 James S. Russell, "Inane Visitor Center Will Wreck Maya Lin's Vietnam Memorial," http://www.bloomberg.com/apps/news?pid=email_en&refer=muse&sid=aTxfitDwplyE, accessed 4 February 2008.

18 Thomas, *The Lincoln Memorial*. See especially the final chapter.

19 Serguisz Michalski, *Public Monuments: Art in Political Bondage 1870-1997*, London: Reaktion, 1999, pp. 108–109.

[12]
Mnemonic Value and Historic Preservation

Jorge Otero-Pailos

Jacques Austerlitz, the fictitious retired professor of architectural history in W. G. Sebald's eponymous novel, was both fascinated and tormented by certain buildings that triggered unsettling memories in him.[1] Austerlitz was "always irresistibly drawn back" to London's old Liverpool Street Station, where his recollections became increasingly vivid with each successive visit. The peak of intensity, and the turning point of the story, came when Austerlitz walked into the disused Ladies' Waiting Room of the station, where he experienced an elaborate flashback in which he saw himself as a child, sitting next to a couple of strangers who would become his parents. The revelation confirmed his suspicions of having been adopted, and sent him on a search for his true identity. In this story, the original function of the station as transportation infrastructure was relegated to a second plane when Austerlitz recognized the building's more critical function as a catalyst for his memory. In his eyes, the station began to function more as a monument, a word derived from the Latin *monumentum*, meaning "that which recalls remembrance," and assists the mind in the act of recollecting the past. Sebald described the emergence of the building's monumental or mnemonic function as something circumscribed within Austerlitz's mind and its return to his repressed past.

[12–1]

EERO SAARINEN,
TWA TERMINAL,
KENNEDY AIRPORT,
NEW YORK, 1962.
[JORGE OTERO-PAILOS]

TODAY, THE TERMINAL
IS WITHOUT PASSENGERS.
DESPITE THE FACT THAT
THE BUILDING CANNOT
ACCOMMODATE
CONTEMPORARY AIR-
LINE TRAVEL, IT WAS
DESIGNATED A NEW
YORK CITY LANDMARK
IN 1994 AND WAS
ALSO LISTED ON THE
NATIONAL REGISTER OF
HISTORIC PLACES IN 2005.

The process of recognizing the mnemonic function of a building can also be a collective process governed by an economy of rules that are institutional, cultural, political, financial, legal, philosophical, and even ideological. The shorthand for that process is known as historic preservation. As a result of these interests, in the public eye the mnemonic value of a building may increase to such a degree that it serves as the sole justification for preserving the structure. In some extreme cases, buildings that become entirely impractical in terms of their original function (for example, old farms, fortresses, customs houses, and pre-jet-age airport terminals) might nevertheless be retained on the grounds that the value of their monumental function outweighs all the site's possible other uses [12–1]. The emergence of mnemonic value was possible within the framework of a powerful nation state capable of regulating financial and real estate markets, and capable of shielding certain buildings from the forces of those markets for the sake of its own representation [12–2]. Historic preservation, like the canary in the mine, is most vulnerable to the waning of the power of nation states over their territories. In the context of globalization, private corporations are gradually drawing the usufruct from the collective value created by historic preservation. To better understand the fundamental transformation that historic preservation is undergoing today, this chapter reconsiders the question of the mnemonic value of places.

As Austerlitz's story unfolds we learn that, much to his chagrin, Liverpool Street Station was partially demolished only weeks after he experienced his epiphany, altered beyond recognition, so that further spatial recall is now impossible. This scene of architectural destruction is an apt preamble to a discussion of how the mnemonic function of buildings is collectively recognized. Despite Austerlitz's deep personal need for the station in the reconstruction of his individual identity, the structure was not declared worthy of historic preservation. Indeed, for a building to become an object of historic preservation its mnemonic function must transcend individual purposes and become useful for constructing a collective identity.

Collective political identity of the sort derived from historic buildings is contingent on the partaking of numerous individuals. But the process through which this affiliation is achieved is neither top-down, obvious, nor overt. The construction of collective political identity through preserved buildings is a much softer and indirect affair—although individual memory plays a big role in it. Yet, ultimately the memory that counts more in shaping collective identity is personal memory and less the recall of historical facts recited by tour guides or written on plaques. It is not that historical facts are unimportant. Historians like James Loewen have exposed the factual errors and appalling distortions that are presented in some historic monuments and sites. This kind of corrective work is an important defense against ideological manipulation. Loewen's effort is all the more critical since, as he notes, the majority of American citizens do not take a national history class after high school, and learn their history of the nation through family trips to monuments at various tourist

[12-2]
**WARREN AND WHITMORE,
WITH REED AND STERN,
GRAND CENTRAL
TERMINAL,
NEW YORK, 1913.**
[MARC TREIB]

AGAINST THE INTENTION
OF ITS OWNER,
PENN CENTRAL
TRANSPORTATION CO.,
TO INCREASE THE REAL
ESTATE VALUE OF THE
SITE BY DEVELOPING
A HIGH RISE TOWER
ABOVE IT, THE BUILDING
WAS DESIGNATED A NEW
YORK CITY LANDMARK
IN 1967.

[12-3]
**GUTZON BORGLUM,
MOUNT RUSHMORE,
NEAR KEYSTONE,
SOUTH DAKOTA,
1927–1941.**
[PUBLIC DOMAIN]

MOUNT RUSHMORE IS
ONE OF THE FAVORITE
DESTINATIONS FOR
AMERICANS ON FAMILY
VACATIONS. PICTURED
HERE IS THE REUNION
OF THE JOHNSON FAMILY
IN 2006.

destinations [12–3].[2] Undoubtedly, trips to historic sites are an important part of most family vacations, but parents do not put themselves through the ordeal of traveling great distances with their children to teach them a series of facts that they could have found more efficiently and economically on the Internet. People visit historic sites for the experience, not the facts. Consumer-oriented societies like that of the United States have been quicker to acknowledge this reality, and the last decade has seen the emergence of the Director of Visitor Experience at prominent historic sites where before there had been only a resident historian.

Despite its importance to most visitors, the question of personal experience is rarely addressed in preservation theory. As a result, experience is not recognized as a critical connection between preservation, memory, and the formation of collective political identity. Instead, the connection between preservation and that identity is understood to hinge on the legal act of designation. In countries with historic preservation laws in effect, the government uses its power to designate those places that should be made to endure and does so for the sake of collective memory, something that it considers a public good.[3] Especially in the United States, a country that prides itself on its multiculturalism, the question of "What collective?" ("Whose memory?") is often hotly debated. For instance, the 2001 addition of Manhattan's Lower East Side district to the National Register of Historic Places was criticized for celebrating only the neighborhood's Jewish immigrant

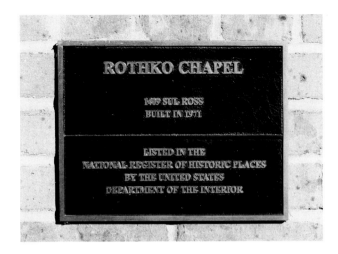

history, to the exclusion of other immigrant groups.[4] Historic preservation theorists like Antoinette Lee have even likened designation to a process through which minorities can gain political visibility, legitimacy, and awareness of their own collective identity.[5]

It is certainly important to scrutinize and contest designations such as these. But by focusing exclusively on the act of designation, preservationists have tended to incorrectly identify the "collective" in "collective memory" as the group that pushed the designation or was cited in the accompanying report. This premise assumes designation celebrates the identity of (local) communities and not the power of the state. If we approach the question of social memory from the perspective of individual experience an entirely different picture emerges: one in which the state continues to figure prominently as the force that holds together and ultimately shapes collective memory.

To speak of personal experience in historic preservation is to shift the focus from the production of historic resources to their reception. The whole purpose of designation is to widen the reception of a building or site by publicly recognizing it as historical, as something that has endured [12–4A, 12–4B]. The language of designation is utilitarian: it names buildings and sites as historic resources, that is, as stocks or reserves to be drawn upon when necessary for the purposes of making history. Designation does not restrict who may draw upon that resource to make history—it could be a trained historian

[12–4A] *opposite*
PHILIP JOHNSON, ROTHKO CHAPEL, HOUSTON, TEXAS, 1971.
[MARC TREIB]

[12–4B] *above*
THE PLAQUE ON THE DOOR OF THE ROTHKO CHAPEL.
[JORGE OTERO-PAILOS]

THE PLAQUE INDICATES A HISTORIC RESOURCE DESIGNATED BY THE UNITED STATES DEPARTMENT OF THE INTERIOR.

employed by the government or an uneducated child. Also, designation does not determine what sort of history should be made from those resources—it could be the history of the nation or a child's personal history. Designation simply names and commits an object to a history yet to be written. What matters is who will write that history, for whom it will have been written, and how the buildings (the so-called facts) will have served in its production.

In recent decades, these questions have been displaced by yet another: whose history? This question is repeated like a mantra every time a designation is ratified—as if to drive all other thoughts from the mind. But this important question implies that the complete history of the site has already been written, and that we are now searching only for its author. It is a search misguided by an inadequate understanding of the intention of designation, which is only to create the resources, the possibility, or the conditions for a future history. The question of "Whose history?" came to American historic preservation in the 1990s from literary criticism, and it was poorly understood and interpreted. Preservationists turned to the designation report for answers. Their search was guided by important questions, such as "Who wrote this report?", "In whose interest?" But they did not stop to ask the fundamental question: Is this report history? When American preservationists looked at their early designation reports from the 1960s, they encountered simple surveys of the physical conditions of the buildings, often no more than a page each. The desire to find history made many preservationists blind to the fact that these reports were not history, properly speaking. They insisted on seeing them as poorly written history which needed to be amended, expanded, referenced, and in short, turned into history. Contemporary designation reports run the length of academic architectural history essays and have the encyclopedic ambition to amass "all" the aesthetic, technological, social, economic, and political histories associated with the site. Thus, contemporary reports collapse production and reception, operating at once as instruments for fabricating historic resources, and as the first, almost instantaneous, histories of those resources.

There are limits to the kind of history that a designation report can become, however. Designation infers public recognition, and therefore it must remain within the bounds of what is public—necessarily excluding private personal histories. In terms of the report, the question of "Whose history?" can only question how that document defines the public, which is understood as the intended audience of the document. This recurring question was motivated by a desire to rectify perceived asymmetries in how the public was implicitly represented in official designations—as a collective restricted to the WASP elite—and the more inclusive definition of the public that community and minority activists claimed should be restored to the process of historic preservation [12–5].

Within historic preservation discourse the designation report serves as the vehicle to transform a building or site into a public monument, in the strict sense of a physical resource from which the public may withdraw the facts of its history. But the public does not, indeed cannot, recall anything. The public is an abstraction. The "public" comprises what is customarily said, believed, and made by people, by anyone; in other words, by no one person in particular. The fact that a building is publicly recognized as a monument in a designation report does not make it function as a monument. For a building to function as a monument a person must experience it as such.

From the perspective of personal experience, a place is not a monument until we return to it. To serve its mnemonic function we must visit it at least twice. We must first have the experience of that place, after which time must intervene in fading our recall of that first exposure. When returning, we relive our memories of that first visit, enhanced by the full vividness of the place where we first lived it. The mnemonic function of places fills the holes in our fragmentary recollections.

In this sense, any place might serve as a monument, regardless of whether or not it is publicly recognized as one. We can have a meaningful experience anywhere. But here is the catch: the places where we can relive our experiences are limited both by the internal circumstances of life (i.e. to the small number of places visited, and the smaller number of places to which we return) and by the external pressures exerted on those places by other people (who might, for instance, decide to develop the farm field where I used to play as a child), or by nature and time. Thus, the enduring places by which to

relive memories are by definition rare, and their value is a function of that endurance and that rarity.

From the perspective of individual experience, publicly designated monuments acquire mnemonic value simply because they endure; not from the public history that is written about them in designation reports. Allow me to indulge in a personal experience to reinforce this point. When I returned to the Lincoln Memorial in Washington, D.C., the stark whiteness of the marble steps, which had been recently cleaned in August 2006, made me recall the ridiculous black-and-yellow-striped tank top that my Uncle John wore when he took me to the building when I was a child [12–6]. Because of the colors his outline stood out against the white steps, making him look like a big fat bee. I also recalled the reprimand I received after telling him about that likeness (he was very sensitive about his weight)—and that I did not learn a thing about Lincoln except that he was thin. What triggered that memory was the whiteness of the building, which had endured. I would not have recalled any of this had not the yellowish streaks of pollution which afflict marble buildings been regularly cleaned from the building during the intervening three decades between my visits. The National Park Service invests dearly in this whiteness: the agency power-washes the statue of Lincoln twice a year. The details of my personal history are not what matter here. More critical is that the Lincoln Memorial increased in value for me as a result of its endurance, rarity, and the mnemonic uses it serves. Significantly, I had nothing to do with the building's endurance. That was the work of the state. But without that investment of state resources, the building would, no doubt, have a reduced mnemonic value. Here, we begin to see how historic preservation imbricates personal memory and the power of the state.

PRIVATE VERSUS PUBLIC

The increase in mnemonic value that I describe is related to, but not coincident with, what the Viennese art historian Alois Riegl (1858–1905) called "age value" in his 1903 essay "The Modern Cult of Monuments." Riegl wrote this document as the basis for a new Austrian legislation for historic preservation, and today it is considered to be one of the foundational texts of modern preservation theory. Age value, for Riegl, was the

[12–5]
SLAVE CABINS,
BOONE HALL
PLANTATION,
CHARLESTON,
SOUTH CAROLINA,
NINETEENTH CENTURY.
[MARC TREIB]

[12–6]
HENRY BACON,
LINCOLN MEMORIAL,
WASHINGTON DC,
1922.
[MARC TREIB]

effect of the uneducated mass public's vague appreciation of monuments simply as objects that had endured the test of time. He thought this valuation of age was emblematic of the modern age, and concomitant with a transformation in the nature of the public, which had spread from a small, highly educated elite to a large, poorly educated mass.[6] The mass public, argued Riegl, possessed only the most basic aesthetic sensibility. It lacked the prerequisite knowledge of history to value the building as a document, a fact, and a link in the great chain of historic evolution. Riegl lamented the decline in the historic value of monuments: "But is it already anachronistic," he asked, "to take into account the historic value [of monuments]?"[7] For the early-twentieth-century Austrian mass public:

> The monument is nothing but the sensible substrate needed to produce that diffuse impression on the spectator caused in modern man by the representation of the necessary cycle of birth and death, of the emergence of the singular from the general, and of its progressive and ineluctable return to the general.[8]

A monument achieves age value from its ability to provide the public with a feeling of memory, without the public's actual recollection of anything specific. Since the quality of memory is a function of its specificity it is understandable that, following Riegl's logic, the enlargement of the public from elites like himself (who used monuments to recall dates and styles) to the mass public (who allegedly used monuments to recall vague ideas of age) signified an important loss in the quality of memory. But I would argue that Riegl's conclusion issued more from his theoretical apparatus than from reality itself. Riegl failed to note that the public is no one in particular, and therefore by definition cannot recall anything, either specific or vague. Identifying himself as a member of the elite public, Riegl made his own personal experiences of the mnemonic function of monuments stand in for how the entire elite public experienced monuments. Incapable of associating himself with the mass public, on the other hand, he began to treat the public as the abstraction it really is, backing into the notion that the public—either mass or elite—cannot recall.

Riegl's meditation on age value stands as an important, albeit unintentional, step towards rethinking the relationship between the individual and the public as a function of the mnemonic uses we make of the objects, and the environments that surround us all. This larger intellectual question, which was quite current in Europe at the dawn of the twentieth century, frames Riegl's thinking. It would take another decade for it to be adequately addressed in philosophy, however. Although this is not the place to discuss the relevant philosophical literature, it is worth mentioning José Ortega y Gasset's *Meditaciones del Quijote* (1914), which described how the appearance of objects is inherently unstable and changes in relation to the life projects of the person experiencing them, and conversely, how personal life projects are determined by the things that surround us. "I am myself and my circumstances," he wrote summing up his analysis. In later works, Ortega y Gasset described the public as something that was ontologically impersonal, a structure of given positions, attitudes and behaviors that individuals could freely take up or reject.[9] Significantly, and more overtly than Riegl, Ortega y Gasset defended the role played by elites in establishing a critical distance vis à vis the positions, opinions, and behaviors present in the public.

Building on the recognition of the difference between the public and the individual, we can also distinguish between age value as an established way of recognizing monuments that pertains to the realm of the public, and mnemonic value as the importance that a place gains for a person when he or she uses it to recollect his or her personal memories. A Marxist analysis would conclude that age value is a form of exchange value, whereas mnemonic value is a form of use value. In *Das Kapital* (1867), Karl Marx argued that the value of an object varies depending on whether it was meant to be consumed privately in the regeneration of one's life, in which case it had use value, or publicly for economic profit, in which case it had exchange value. Marx has been faulted by his critics for believing that use value was an objective "absolute value" rooted in human labor, the biological effort of staying alive. In the early 1950s, Hannah Arendt argued that such "absolute values" do not exist. She explained that the very notion of "value" presupposed "universal relativity, that a thing exists only in relation to other things, and loss of intrinsic worth, that nothing any longer possesses an 'objective' value independent of the ever-changing estimations of supply and demand."[10]

Value, in other words, is an idea of the proportion between the desire for one thing versus the drive to possess another, and always concerns value in the process of exchange. For Arendt, everything, from human bodily labor to the work of making goods necessary for the life of the body, only acquires value once it is brought to the market where everything can be exchanged for something else—where all things are esteemed, demanded, or neglected depending on what else is available in the marketplace. "Value," she wrote, "is the quality a thing can never possess in privacy but acquires automatically the moment it appears in public."[11]

Arendt's analysis allows us to further nuance our description of mnemonic value. Strictly speaking, mnemonic value cannot be private. My personal experience of the mnemonic function of a place, insofar as it remains private, cannot give value to that place. Rather, it increases the meaning of that place for me personally: the place's mnemonic function makes it significant to me. I recognize it as the outward expression of my interior recollections. But that meaning cannot have value because, unlike the place itself, the personal meaning of the place cannot be used to achieve something else, or exchanged for something else. The meaning that the place holds for me is intrinsic and unique to it. From a utilitarian point of view, the meaning of the place can only be a worthless end in itself.

Here we come to the crux of the question concerning how the private mnemonic meaning becomes transformed into a public mnemonic value. The mnemonic value of a place requires a process of reification, whereby personal remembrance is transformed into an object of memory. The process only seems natural. I activate the mnemonic function of a place when I recognize my memories there. Then a process of transference begins, through which I begin to identify my memory, some-thing immaterial, with the material place. As a result of this reification, I come to identify the place as something that replaces myself as the vessel of my innermost thoughts. Sebald provides a vivid description of this process when he narrates how Jacques Austerlitz, recognizing his childhood memories in yet another train station, wondered if the building contained his memories irrespective of him:

What made me uneasy at the sight of it, however, was not
how the complex form of the capital, now covered with a
puce-tinged encrustation, had really impressed itself on
my mind when I passed through Pilsen with the children's
transport in the summer of 1939, but the idea, ridiculous
in itself, that this cast iron column, which with its scaly
surface seemed almost to approach the nature of a living
being, might remember me and was, if I may so put it,
said Austerlitz, a witness to what I could no longer recol-
lect for myself.[12]

This passage conveys how the experience of buildings
helps recall our memories, but also, and more disturbingly,
confronts us with the holes in our memory, with what we
cannot recall. As I locate the fragments of my memory of a
place within it, the remainder falls silent. That silent fabric
presses against me with the fullness of reality, yet I experience
it as lacking content, something empty of meaning. In an
uncanny reversal, what becomes significant is not what I
recognize, but what I do not apprehend, for it begins to reorgan-
ize the fragments of my memory according to its own logic,
helping me make connections that I could not have imagined,
and holding out the promise of further revelations.

ENDURANCE

Mnemonic values emerge from the differences between what
I can and cannot recall. That the place has endured guarantees
its worth, in contrast to the disintegration of my memory. That
is to say, mnemonic value derives from the fact that it has
endured. Because it has endured, I can use the place to help
me recall what I have forgotten. When we attribute mnemonic
value to a place we look upon it in a utilitarian fashion, in the
sense that we regard the place merely as an instrument for us
to achieve something else: a private recollection.

The existence of historic preservation as a practice testi-
fies to the fact that places do not endure, but are constantly
transformed to accommodate the changing requirements of
our lives. Left alone they suffer damage by nature and fall
to ruin. If endurance is the power that holds the self-same
appearance of a place in time, then we must recognize that
endurance itself is wholly artificial. For a place to endure
requires ongoing financial investment in its preservation

[12–7]. But a fiscal intervention alone yields no mnemonic value; in addition we require the psychological investment of our personal memories. Financial and psychological investment rarely endure together over the long period of time required to yield mnemonic value from a place. Ancestral family homes, handed down through generations, are such singular examples. But most of us did not grow up in such homes. We have no guarantee that our psychological investment in places will be met with the resources required to continue their existence. Our memories of place are at the mercy of the real estate market—except where historic preservation is at work.

Preservation is usually associated with the state's power to subjugate and control private actions. The analysis is not entirely incorrect but it is unnecessarily restricted to the viewpoint of the law, to the restrictions imposed by designation. From the perspective of personal memory, historic preservation involves an entirely different form of state power. The return to a historic site does not reveal the power of the state in the same way as receiving a speeding ticket, or being denied entry at a nation's border. Preservation does not generate an experience of repression, but instead, an experience of endurance. More precisely it demonstrates the power of the state to sustain its built heritage, and ultimately to demonstrate the endurance of the state itself. The mnemonic value of historic places is contingent on the state's power to make them last beyond their original functional viability. The state's long-term financial outlays in the preservation of historic places makes possible the psychological investment of visitors over their lifetime, and guarantees the endurance of the place long enough for it to yield its public mnemonic value.

Significantly, when we return to a place preserved by the state to recall our memories we cannot divorce our recollections from the experience of the state's power to make that place endure. Historic preservation reveals itself as the instrument through which the state exhibits its power to endure within the meaningful context of personal experience. These memories are most effective in the ideological construction of collective political identity precisely because they pertain to our personal identity, and on the surface they seem to have nothing to do with political affiliation. Historic preservation creates the material and politically charged stage for the reification of personal memory, and then offers it back to us in the guise of collective political identity, such that the memories that make up our own personal identity appear to us inextricably bound with that of the state.

EXCHANGE

If one aspect of historic preservation ensures mnemonic value (understood as personal meaning), a second aspect concerns its entrance into the public marketplace. Endurance, it should be recalled, is also a necessary condition for the production of exchange value. As Arendt noted, in order to enter the market commodities must be more permanent than the activity which produced them.[13]

Hand in hand with the massification of cultural tourism in the twentieth century, mass advertising has employed the publicly recognized mnemonic value of historic places to sell tourism services. To sell transportation tickets or hotel accommodations, by the early 1920s advertisers had begun experimenting with posters featuring beautifully rendered images of well-known monuments. These were the early days of so-called "product placement" in which advertisers sought to increase the exchange value of products by placing them in the meaningful context of iconic monuments. By trial and error, those advertisers perfected the art of product placement. One of the famously unintentional breakthroughs was the scene in the film *It Happened One Night* (1934) in which Clark Gable took off his shirt to expose his bare chest —sales of men's undershirts plummeted. Like Clark Gable, cultural icons like the Alhambra can attract the popular attention. Their mnemonic value evokes feelings and emotions, for example, that can influence purchasing behavior. The technique of product placement also makes the public nature of mnemonic value clear. The memories we might expect to have at mature historic sites may actually precede our experience on site. They exist there, publicly—inherited from previous generations, untraceable to any one person's own experience—an impersonal behavior, an established way of remembering a place that can be taken up and made our own. The clichéd pose that tourists assume before the Leaning Tower of Pisa (in order to appear in their photographs as if they are propping it up) suggests that responses to historic places replicate on-site images established in the mind long before [12–8]. The novelist Don DeLillo expressed the feeling brought about by our acceptance of the established mnemonic value of a place:

> Being here is kind of a spiritual surrender. We see only what the others see. The thousands who were here in the past, those who will come in the future. We've agreed to be part of a collective perception. This literally colors our vision. A religious experience in a way, like all tourism.[14]

By the 1960s, the governments of the United Kingdom, France, Singapore, and others hired David Ogilvy, the legendary advertising executive, to increase tourism revenues. His formula used pictures of sites with high mnemonic value, places that were unique. "People," he wrote, "don't go halfway around the world to see things they can equally well see at home."[15] To advertise Britain, for instance, he showed a "mouth watering" picture of Westminster Abbey. Today, the tourism industry carefully monitors the public appeal of monuments around the world. Times Square, in New York City, tops the list of most visited sites in the world, with 35 million people per year, followed by Washington D.C.'s Mall and memorial parks, which draw 25 million visitors.[16]

Advertisers have come to recognize that some monuments attract larger audiences than some television shows.

Private companies vie to use the most famous world monuments as media devices through which to present and broadcast their brands in a meaningful context of memorable vacations. At the moment, a huge billboard partially hiding the facade of the Milan cathedral is rented out to advertisers like Camper Shoes and Vagari Watches, for example [12–9]. To allay the frustration of tourists, some explanatory posters at ground level explain that the billboards are only temporary, and will be removed when the conservation work is completed. In other words: preservation campaigns have become advertising campaigns.

Benefiting from the fact that cash-strapped governments are increasingly unable to maintain even their most famous monuments, private companies are stepping in to finance preservation work. American Express awards yearly preservation grants to historic places around the world. In exchange for sponsoring the preservation of monuments, American Express receives the right to present its logo at the site, in the meaningful context of what their consumers care about. Down the line, governments still must pay for these private investments in public preservation when they are deducted from their balance sheets as tax deductions. But, I would argue, the state pays an even higher price. Compared to what governments invest annually in historic preservation, the sums that private companies invest are only a pittance. Shrewdly, they invest only in those monuments and aspects of preservation that will yield the highest return on investment. Conservation campaigns are the most visible physical manifestations of the state's power to make places endure—they are only the tip of the iceberg, however. By encouraging private companies to literally put their flags on it, the state's power to endure appears symbolically weakened. As the instrument of this weakening effect, historic preservation shows itself to be part of the greater process of globalization, which is but a collective dream of the demise of the nation state. We are perhaps not far from wish fulfillment: It turns out that the 2006 cleaning of the Lincoln Memorial steps that I so dearly remembered was actually organized and financed by Goodyear Engineered Products and DeWalt Pressure Washers.

NOTES

1 W. G. Sebald, *Austerlitz*, London: Penguin Books, 2001.

2 James W. Loewen, *Lies Across America: What Our Historic Sites Get Wrong*, New York: Simon & Schuster, 1999.

3 To be precise, designation can be made by more than a single governing body, as is evident in the various types of overlapping designations that exist, and that may coexist in a single building. In the United States they include national, state, and city designations, each regulated by a different level of government. In Europe, designations are national, although some regional governments have achieved sufficient power to create and regulate their own separate registries.

4 See Randall Mason and Max Page, "Rethinking the Roots of the Historic Preservation Movement," in *Giving Preservation a History: Histories of Historic Preservation in the United States*, Max Page and Randall Mason, eds, Oxon: Routledge, 2004, pp. 3–4.

5 Antoinette Lee, "From Historic Preservation to Cultural Heritage: A Journey Through Diversity, Identity, and Community," *Future Anterior*, vol. 1, n. 2, (Fall 2004), pp. 15–23.

6 Alois Riegl, *Le Culte Moderne des Monuments: Son Essence et sa Genèse*, 1903, trans. Daniel Wieczorek, reprint Paris: Éditions du Seuil, 1984, p. 57.

7 Ibid., p. 76.

8 Ibid, p. 46.

9 See especially José Ortega y Gasset, *La Rebelión de las Masas* (1930) and *En Torno a Galileo* (1942).

10 Hannah Arendt, *The Human Condition*, Chicago: Univeristy of Chicago Press, 1958, p. 166.

11 Ibid., p. 164.

12 Sebald, *Austerlitz*, p. 311.

13 Arendt, *The Human Condition*, p. 136.

14 Don DeLillo, *White Noise*, New York: Penguin Books, 1985.

15 David Ogilvy, *Ogilvy on Advertising*, New York: Vintage Books, 1985, p. 130.

16 Sandra Larriva and Gabe Weisert, "Forbes Traveler 50 Most Visited Tourist Attractions," in *Forbes Traveler Online*, 25 April 2007, http://www.forbestraveler.com/best-lists/most-visited-tourist-attractions-story.html, accessed 7 June 2008.

[12–9]
A HUGE BILLBOARD IN FRONT OF THE MILAN CATHEDRAL TURNS HISTORIC PRESERVATION WORK INTO AN OPPORTUNITY FOR AN ADVERTISING CAMPAIGN.
[PUBLIC DOMAIN]

Acknowledgments

The original symposium, "Spatial Recall: The Place of Memory in Architecture and Landscape," was held in March 2007, sponsored by the College of Environmental Design at the University of California, Berkeley. For the financial resources, and for fully supporting the program, I need to thank former Dean Harrison Fraker. The Townsend Center for the Humanities also provided additional funding, for which we are grateful. The event would never have run smoothly without the help of the late Sameera Sutton in the College of Environmental Design Dean's office. She deftly handled most of the practical issues, among them arranging the logistics for the speakers, answering calls for information, and planning the breaks and reception from which we all benefited. I would also like to express my gratitude to Stephen Suh and Kari Holmquist for developing and maintaining the website despite continued requests for modification.

Credits for the images in the book are given in each caption, but I would here like to thank these individuals and institutions collectively.

At Routledge, I again (for the fourth time) thank former Sponsoring Editor Caroline Mallinder, who took this project on; Katherine Morton, who managed the editing and production skillfully and with aplomb (also fourth time), Sarah Fish for focused copyediting; and Amanda Lastoria for meticulous proof reading. They were a wonderful team to work with.

Contributors

Alice Aycock's numerous sculptural installations include commissions for the San Francisco Public Library; *East River Roundabout*, New York City; and *Ghost Ballet for the East Bank Machineworks*, Nashville, Tennessee (2007). In 2005 the MIT Press published the first major monograph on her work: *Alice Aycock, Sculpture and Projects*, authored by Robert Hobbs.

Esther da Costa Meyer, Associate Professor in Art History at Princeton University, specializes in European and American architecture of the nineteenth, twentieth, and twenty-first centuries. She is the author of *The Work of Sant'Elia*, a study of the drawings of Frank Gehry, and is currently completing a social history of the urban transformation of Paris during the Second Empire.

Georges Descombes, Professor Emeritus of Architecture, University of Geneva, works as both architect and landscape architect. His designs are characterized by an intensive investigation of the qualities and history of the site, deriving their vocabularies from the existing characteristics of the place. Current projects include the Parc de la Cour du Maroc in Paris, a riverfront park in Lyon, and the transformation of the River Aire outside Geneva.

Adriaan Geuze, founding partner of West 8, based in Rotterdam, is regarded as one of Europe's leading landscape architects and urban designers, with numerous projects in the Netherlands, the United Kingdom, and other countries. In addition to professional practice he has lectured and taught at many schools in the United States and abroad.

Matt Kondolf, Professor of Environmental Planning at the University of California, Berkeley, is a geomorphologist and hydrologist who conducts research on river evolution, the effects of human activities on river channels, and the ecological restoration of rivers. Recent research topics include the management of Mediterranean-climate rivers in California and Europe, and the restoration of the Sacramento and Mississippi river deltas.

Luigi Latini, who received his PhD in landscape architecture from the University of Florence, works as both a researcher and landscape architect. He is the author of numerous publications on cemeteries and modern landscape architecture and currently serves as Adjunct Professor of Landscape Architecture at the University of Venice's IUAV.

Donlyn Lyndon, Professor of Architecture at the University of California, Berkeley, is the editor of the journal *Places* and an architect concerned with how built works engage the life around them and the specific places of which they are a part. He is the author of numerous articles and publications including *Chambers for a Memory Palace* (1994), co-authored with Charles Moore, and *The Sea Ranch* (2004).

Jorge Otero-Pailos, Assistant Professor of Historic Preservation at Columbia University, is an architect and theorist whose works and articles have been featured in publications such as *Artforum*, *Architectural Record*, and *AA Files*. He is the founder and editor of *Future Anterior*—a scholarly journal of preservation history, theory, and criticism—and currently serves as the vice-president of DoCoMoMo US.

Juhani Pallasmaa, Professor Emeritus of Architecture at the Helsinki University of Technology, has practiced architecture and exhibition, product, and graphic design since the early 1960s. He has served as the director of the Museum of Finnish Architecture and dean of the Department of Architecture at the Helsinki University of Technology. He has written or edited numerous books and countless essays, and has received many awards for his buildings and contributions to architecture.

Susan Schwartzenberg is a visual artist whose wide-ranging subjects of interest include biography, memory, urban life, and the psychology of place. Her projects have been realized as books, installations, curated exhibitions, and public art works. In 1998–99 she was a recipient of the Loeb Fellowship for Advanced Environmental Studies from Harvard University. As Senior Artist at the Exploratorium in San Francisco she has instigated a series of exhibitions on the science and art of human memory.

Andrew Shanken, Assistant Professor of Architectural History at the University of California, Berkeley, teaches courses on American architecture and urbanism, memorials, and anti-modernism, and has published several key articles on the subject of the memorial in contemporary America. His book *194X*, recently published, studies wartime architecture, planning, and consumer culture on the American home front.

Marc Treib is Professor of Architecture Emeritus at the University of California, Berkeley, a practicing graphic designer, and an active author with numerous books and articles on the subjects of landscape architecture, graphic design, and modern and historical architecture. Recent books include *Settings and Stray Paths: Writings on Landscapes and Gardens* (2005), *Representing Landscape Architecture* (2007), *Appropriate: The Houses of Joseph Esherick*, and *Thinking/Drawing: Confronting an Electronic Age* (both 2008).

Index